The Economics of Addictive Behaviours Volume II

John Joshua

The Economics of Addictive Behaviours Volume II

The Private and Social Costs of the Abuse of Alcohol and Their Remedies

palgrave
macmillan

John Joshua
Deakin University
Melbourne, Victoria, Australia

ISBN 978-3-319-54424-3 ISBN 978-3-319-54425-0 (eBook)
DOI 10.1007/978-3-319-54425-0

Library of Congress Control Number: 2016954960

Printed on acid-free paper

This Palgrave Macmillan imprint is published by Springer Nature
The registered company is Springer International Publishing AG
The registered company address is: Gewerbestrasse 11, 6330 Cham, Switzerland

'To my beloved wife Feng Yan for her continuing compassion and understanding over many years'

CONTENTS

1 Introduction 1

2 The Worldwide Consumption of Alcohol 5
1 Introduction 5

3 The Causes and Stages of Alcohol Abuse: From Initiation to Alcohol Dependence 11
1 Introduction 11

4 The Consequences of Alcohol Abuse 19
1 Introduction 19

5 The Prevention and Treatment of Alcohol Abuse 37
1 Introduction 37

6 Legal Remedies to Reduce Alcohol Consumption 49
1 Introduction 49

7 The Market and the Social and Private Costs of Alcohol Abuse 59
1 Introduction 59

8 Economic Remedies to Reduce Alcohol Abuse 73
1 Elasticities and the Demand for Alcohol 74

2 Taxation Policies to Reduce the Abuse of Alcohol 80
3 Minimum Price Policies and the Abuse of Alcohol 90

9 The Politics of Corporate and Social Responsibilities 93
1 Corporate Social Responsibilities and Policies 94
2 Corporate Responsibilities and Social Costs 95

10 Conclusion 101

References 103

Index 119

List of Figures

Fig. 3.1	The four different phase of alcohol use	12
Fig. 3.2	The pathways from initiation to chronic and acute diseases	15
Fig. 4.1	The anxiolytic use of alcohol	32
Fig. 8.1	Effects of an excise tax when absorbed by producer	75
Fig. 8.2	Effects of an excise tax when passed on to consumers	76

CHAPTER 1

Introduction

Abstract This is the second volume of a four-volume series entitled "The Economics of Addictive Behaviours". As behavioural diseases are essentially multidisciplinary, this book takes a multidisciplinary approach. This book describes the patterns of the consumption of alcohol and the worldwide risk factors of alcohol abuse. The causes and the stages of alcohol abuse from initiation to alcohol dependence, including the chronic and acute diseases and social problems which may follow from alcohol abuse, are discussed followed with the prevention and treatment of alcohol abuse. Legal remedies to reduce the abuse of alcohol, and economic remedies, including the elasticities and the demand for alcohol, taxation policies and minimum price policies are discussed in details followed with a discussion of corporate and social responsibilities.

Keywords Behavioural diseases · Economic policies · Alcohol as a psychoactive drug · Alcohol abuse and dependence

The studies of behavioural diseases are essentially multidisciplinary and so are the solutions to problems of addiction. Various disciplines are able to complement each other in any understanding of behavioural diseases. Like smoking, the use of illicit drugs and overeating, the consumption of alcohol is a matter of lifestyle for many; indeed, alcohol and nicotine are the most widely abused drugs. The impact of the four types of lifestyle

J. Joshua, *The Economics of Addictive Behaviours Volume II*,
DOI 10.1007/978-3-319-54425-0_1

behaviour as discussed in these four volumes is considerable in terms of social costs and the development of diseases.

The costs and consequences of such four behavioural diseases are substantial in terms of epidemiological, economic and social effects and are described in the four volumes of "The Economics of Behavioural Diseases". This volume is the second volume and describes the "Abuse of Alcohol: The Private and Social Costs and Their Remedies". Economic policies can make a vital contribution towards the reduction in the abuse of alcohol as they may reduce the consumption as well as the supply of alcohol and thereby may also increase the effectiveness of policies to reduce the detrimental effects of alcohol abuse.

Alcohol is a psychoactive drug; however, in contrast to other psychoactive drugs, alcohol has been widely culturally accepted in Western countries, except in isolated situations for a short time, it has been legally widely available. Alcohol is one of the most used drugs and is highly detrimental to health. Policies to reduce the abuse of alcohol may operate on the supply and demand side of alcohol; whereas programmes of preventions and treatment operate on the demand side of alcohol abuse, legislations are directed at the supply side of alcohol; that is, it deals with the marketing mix: product, promotion, point of sales and price.

The first chapter provides a general overview of what will be discussed in this book on the abuse of alcohol and its remedies.

The second chapter is divided into two sections: (a) the patterns of the consumption of alcohol and (b) the worldwide risk factors of alcohol abuse. The first section is an overview of the worldwide consumption of alcohol. The second section describes the detrimental effects on health of alcohol abuse. The abuse of alcohol accounts for about 4.0% of deaths worldwide and 4.65% of diseases and injuries.

Chapter 3 explains the causes and stages of alcohol abuse: from initiation to alcohol dependence, and is divided into two sections: (a) living conditions and alcohol abuse and (b) the pathways from initiation to alcohol dependence. Various conditions, including living conditions and socio-demographics which may contribute towards the abuse of alcohol, will also be explained. The association between unemployment, suicide and abuse of alcohol is also described. Users of alcohol may go through different stages; that is, from the initiation to alcohol dependence. Each of the stages requires different types of interventions which are described. The abuse of alcohol may eventually lead to chronic and acute diseases and chronic and acute social problems.

The fourth chapter describes the detrimental consequences of alcohol abuse. This chapter is divided into three sections: (a) the physiological effects of alcohol abuse; (b) the psychosocial effects of alcohol abuse and (c) the processes of alcohol abuse and dependence.

A detailed description is provided of alcohol dependence and alcohol abuse, including a discussion on the American Psychiatric Association's use of such terms in their DSM-IV and DSM-5. The association between alcohol abuse, car accidents, aggression, unemployment and suicide is also discussed. The physical and psychological processes involved in causing numerous detrimental effects will be analysed, including a description of the consequences, such as the Korsakoff–Wernicke syndromes and the effects of the consumption of alcohol during pregnancy. In the last section of this chapter, the problem of self-medication through the abuse of alcohol is also discussed in details.

The fifth chapter deals with the prevention and treatment of alcohol abuse. This chapter consists of five sections which describe the following: (a) government intervention in the abuse of alcohol, (b) the effectiveness in the intervention of the abuse of alcohol, (c) the treatment of alcohol abuse, (d) the prevention and rehabilitation of alcohol abuse and (e) harm minimization as a viable strategy. It will be argued that programmes and government policies should be evaluated using cumulative scientific evidence to determine the appropriate allocation of resources. The treatment of alcohol abuse will also be described, including pharmacogenetics.

The sixth chapter will discuss in details the legal remedies available to reduce the abuse of alcohol. This chapter is divided in five sections: (a) educational impact on the reduction of alcohol abuse; (b) conditions of sales: purchasing outlets, number of locations and density and hours of opening; (c) price promotion and discounts; (d) randomized breath testing and other means to prevent driving under the influence and (e) ban of advertising of alcoholic beverages.

Policies may be directed towards behavioural modification directed at individual alcohol abusers, such as remedies against driving under the influence; or they may be directed at the public at large, such as a ban on advertisements of alcoholic beverages. Such policies could be used together for better effects. However, educational interventions have been largely ineffective.

The seventh chapter deals with the market of alcoholic beverages and the social and private costs of alcohol abuse. This chapter is divided into two sections as follows: (a) international trade and public health and

(b) the social and private costs of alcohol abuse. The first section will discuss the effects of the market and international trade agreements on public health. It will be argued that consumers lack much of the relevant information about the consumption of alcohol to enable them to make rational choices. It will also be argued that various international trade agreements prevent the introduction of viable health policies. The second section will draw from various epidemiological studies and will assess the social and private costs of alcohol abuse, including ways to evaluate such costs. It may put drug policies into a proper perspective as the costs deriving from the abuse of alcohol are in many cases greater than those of illicit drugs.

The eighth chapter will discuss the economic remedies to reduce alcohol abuse. This chapter is divided in three sections as follows: (a) elasticities and the demand for alcohol; (b) taxation policies to reduce the abuse of alcohol and (c) minimum price policies and the abuse of alcohol. The first section is a detailed analysis on the various types of elasticities which affect the demand of alcohol and thus will affect any economic policies that may be used to reduce the abuse of alcohol. The second section provides a detailed analysis of the economic remedies, including taxation policies to reduce alcohol abuse. The third section will discuss minimum price policies and the abuse of alcohol.

The ninth chapter discusses the politics of corporate and social responsibilities of the alcohol companies. This chapter is divided into two sections: (a) corporate social responsibilities and policies and (b) corporate responsibilities and social costs.

The consumption of alcohol is greatly increased by various strategies of marketing. The alcohol industry rejects marketing regulations and instead advocates self-regulation which however has been shown to be ineffective. As their marketing strategies have been quite successful in increasing demand for alcoholic beverages, it has also increased the private and social costs as a result.

The last chapter provides the conclusion which summarizes the main points of the arguments about the private and social costs of the abuse of alcohol and their remedies.

CHAPTER 2

The Worldwide Consumption of Alcohol

Abstract This chapter describes the worldwide consumption of alcohol and the detrimental effect on health. The chapter discusses the patterns of the consumption of alcohol, and the worldwide risk factors of alcohol abuse. Alcohol is widely consumed within developed countries, but it is not an ordinary commodity as it is a toxin. Alcoholic beverages include ethyl alcohol so that alcohol is an addictive psychotropic drug. Terms such as binge drinking, alcohol misuse and alcohol abuse relating to the patterns of alcohol use and their effects on health are also explained. It is argued here that it is the drinking patterns which is more important rather than the volume of alcohol consumed.

Keywords Effect on health · Patterns of consumption · Psychoactive drugs · Consumption · Worldwide risk factors · Disability-adjusted life · Alcohol abuse

1 Introduction

This chapter describes the worldwide consumption of alcohol and the detrimental effect on health. The chapter is divided in two sections: (a) the patterns of the consumption of alcohol and (b) the worldwide risk factors of alcohol abuse.

Terms such as binge drinking, alcohol misuse and alcohol abuse relating to the patterns of alcohol use and their effects on health are also

J. Joshua, *The Economics of Addictive Behaviours Volume II*,
DOI 10.1007/978-3-319-54425-0_2

explained. It is argued here that it is the drinking patterns which is more important rather than the volume of alcohol consumed. Alcoholic beverages include ethyl alcohol so that alcohol is an addictive psychotropic drug.

The Patterns of the Consumption of Alcohol

The alcohol which is part of alcoholic beverages is ethyl alcohol, also known as ethanol. Ethanol is the main psychoactive ingredient in alcoholic beverages; however, the use of "alcohol" is also used to refer to alcoholic beverages. The World Health Organization (2004b) stated that definitions of what constitute an alcoholic beverage range from 0.1% to 12% alcohol by volume. A standard drink generally contains approximately 12.5 ml of alcohol. Low consumption of alcohol of about eight standard drinks of alcohol each week is the optimum level to get the health benefit; however beyond this level, there is an increasing risk of mortality (see Foster and Marriott, 2006). However, alcohol consumption is more associated with morbidity rather than with mortality.

A standard unit of alcohol in the United Kingdom is between 8 g and 10 ml of pure alcohol. The UK government guideline of sensible drinking was 3–4 units of alcohol for men and 2–3 units for women per day (see Foster and Marriott, 2006). However, the guidelines have changed in 2016 when the UK Chief Medical Officers' Alcohol Guideline states that for men and women, to keep health risks from the drinking of alcohol at a safe level, consumers should not drink more than 14 units a week on a regular basis to be spread evenly over at least 3 days and recommend that male and females should on average not drink more than 2 units per day. One unit is the equivalent of 10 ml of pure alcohol (Department of Health, 2016). Most countries still have different guidelines for men and women.

Binge drinking is defined as when at least the double amount is consumed as defined by the sensible drinking guideline, that is, at least 6 and 8 units per day for women and men, respectively (Foster and Marriott, 2006, p. 319). Women are generally more vulnerable to the risk of consuming alcohol as they achieve a higher blood alcohol concentration because of generally lower body weight, higher proportion of body fat and the smaller capacity of their liver to metabolize alcohol.

As alcohol is the second most energy dense nutrient, moderate-to-heavy alcohol consumption may lead to obesity, especially as alcohol is consumed in addition to the usual energy intake through food consumption. However, the meaning of a standard drink may differ between countries. Binge drinking is defined as consisting of five or more standard drinks during a single drinking session (World Health Organization, 2004b). The terms "misuse" and "abuse" of alcohol are often used interchangeably, as they both lead towards hazardous consequences.

Research by Bobak et al. (2004) showed that alcohol consumption per se did not lead to alcohol-induced problems at the population level, but rather the prevalence of binge drinking. Thus their study showed that Russians had a relatively low volume of drinking but had the highest alcohol-related problems, while Russian men consumed 71 g of alcohol per drinking session, Polish men consumed 46 g; however, Russian men had a lower level of alcohol per year at 4.6 l, while Polish men consumed 4.1 l of alcohol. Russian men also had the highest rate of problem drinking (35%) and negative consequence (18%), whereas Poles had 14% of drinking problems and 8% of negative consequences. In their research, binge drinking was related to alcohol problems so that the drinking patterns related strongly to alcohol-related problems. Hence, to reduce the detrimental effects of alcohol consumption, attention has to be paid to the drinking patterns rather than just to the volume of alcohol consumed.

Alcohol is widely consumed within the European Community, but it is not an ordinary commodity (Barbor et al., 2010). It is a toxin, an addictive psychotropic drug and an intoxicant. Alcohol consumption is the highest in economically developed countries, and alcohol is the most used and abused drug. However, there is also a considerable difference in the consumption of alcohol by consumers. The largest differences between genders in the consumption of alcohol are in developing countries and the smallest differences are in the northern European countries. Generally, the greater is the social inequality between genders, the greater the difference between genders in their drinking behaviour (see Bloomfield et al., 2006).

The worldwide per capita consumption by adults varies; the average is about 6.13 l and it is about 10.55 l in high-income countries (World Health Organization, 2011); for example, in England, the heaviest 10% of drinkers consumed about 45% of the alcohol, the heaviest 20% consumed about 60% and the heaviest 30% consumed about 79%. On the other hand, the lightest 40% consumers only consumed about 2% of the total alcohol consumption (Meier et al., 2009, p. 385). However, the distribution of alcohol consumption is more extreme with younger people of the age between 18 and 24-year olds. Amongst males, 59% of alcohol was consumed by the heaviest drinkers of 10%, and for females, it was 37% of all alcohol consumption (p. 385). Different groups also consumed different types of alcohol; for example, of the total alcohol consumption of young men, 68% was beer, and wine and spirit accounted for only 7% each. Amongst women, 57% of their alcohol consumption consisted of wine, 18% consisted of spirits and 17% was beer.

Burki (2010) pointed out that in Germany, "10% of drinkers are responsible for 50% of consumption" (p. 153). Heavy drinkers generally drink the cheapest alcohol, and the imposition of excise taxes is highly effective in reducing the consumption of alcohol. Even though the consumption has been relatively stable for the adult population from the 1990s onwards, it has been increasing for adolescents and younger people. Similarly, in Australia, young Australians start to drink earlier, and their prevalence of drinking is increasing (Degenhardt et al., 2000). However, as more than half of the global population does not consume alcohol, data on the average consumption of alcohol are rather meaningless. The increase in the average consumption occurred concurrently with an increase in affordability (Burki, 2010). Mäkelä (1999a, b) also found that greater affordability increases the use of alcohol, especially amongst the lower socio-economic groups.

The consumption of alcoholic beverages may increase because of an increase in the purchasing power and because of economic and social developments. Economic recession and other social dislocations are more likely to increase detrimental harm caused by the consumption of alcohol (Blomgren et al., 2004). On the other hand, when income falls, the alcohol consumption may fall if alcohol becomes less affordable (Rabinovich et al., 2009).

Alcohol consumption fluctuates worldwide; the highest level of alcohol consumption occurs in the developed countries, whereas the lowest level of consumption occurs in the South-East Asian Region and the Eastern Mediterranean Region. Worldwide, almost 24.8% of consumed alcohol is unrecorded alcohol, especially in the Islamic states of the Eastern Mediterranean (almost 100%) and in the South-East Asian Region (World Health Organization, 2014, p. 30).

There has been a decline to some extent in the consumption of alcohol in heavily drinking countries from the 1970s, while the consumption has been increasing in various emerging countries with an increase of the alcohol per capita consumption of the proportion of heavy drinkers, and the prevalence also increases together with the detrimental effect caused by the abuse of alcohol.

The Worldwide Risk Factors of Alcohol Abuse

The general life expectancy in advanced countries has until more recently increased; however, the threats to health nowadays often come from behavioural diseases caused by style of living rather than from infectious diseases. Alcohol is the more used and abused drug. Amongst 26 risk factors, alcohol is the third highest contributor to disability-adjusted life years (DALYs) (Ezzati et al., 2004). Alcohol-specific mortality has been increasing in 15 European countries (Ramstedt, 2002). The consumption of alcohol is the second largest risk factor for morbidity in high-income countries. The abuse of alcohol caused 2.3 million deaths and 69.4 million DALYs worldwide; for example, the misuse of alcohol is the second behind tobacco in the preventable cause of death and hospitalization in Australia (Commonwealth Department of Health and Aged Care, 2001). DALYs is a measure that combines number of years lost as compared with life expectancy and premature death with number of years lost as a result of disability. The higher the DALYs, the healthier a person is.

Over 30 diseases are attributable sole to alcohol. Alcohol use disorder is the most important disease which includes alcohol abuse and alcohol dependence; in most cases, they are less total than other conditions of chronic diseases (World Health Organization, 2007). The International Classification of Diseases lists various diseases which are attributable partly to the consumption of alcohol such as infectious diseases, various forms of cancer, diabetes, neuropsychiatric diseases, cardiovascular diseases, liver and pancreas diseases and injuries, both intentional and unintentional. The abuse of alcohol together with tobacco is the main cause of preventable cause of mortality. The abuse of alcohol causes approximately 4.0% of deaths worldwide and 4.65% of injury and diseases. Alcohol abuse may cause various chronic diseases such as coronary heart diseases, tuberculoses, breast cancer, liver cirrhoses, as well as acute social problems, such as car accidents and suicide.

Of all causes contributing to ill health and premature death, 4.6% was attributed to the misuse of alcohol worldwide, whereby the poor countries and poorer population carried the greatest burden of alcohol attributed diseases per litre of alcohol consumption (Rehm et al., 2009, pp. 2223–2233). Alcohol abuse contributed an estimated 7.1% of all deaths and 7.0% of total DALYs (deaths and disability-adjusted life years) in 2000 (Schneider et al., 2007). They also found that alcohol abuse contributed 39.0% to interpersonal violence, 18.4% to neuropsychiatric conditions and 14.3% to road traffic injuries (pp. 668–670).

In 2012, 5.9% of all deaths or 3.3 million of all deaths worldwide were attributed to the use of alcohol and 5.1% of global diseases and injury. Globally, 30% of mortality caused by violence has been attributed to alcohol abuse (Ezzati et al., 2006). Twenty per cent of the deaths which has been attributed to alcohol worldwide involved cancer, 22% involved cardiovascular diseases and 27% involved unintentional injuries (Manafò and Giesbrecht, 2011, p. 7). The consumption of alcohol is part of many cultures and has become normalized as part of most people's lifestyles so that it has not received as much attention as other drugs. Twenty-three per cent of Canadian consumers of alcohol are drinking alcohol at levels above low-risk drinking guidelines which is no more than 2 standard drinks or 13.6 g of alcohol per day or 14 standard drinks per week for males and 9 per week for females (Manafò and Giesbrecht, 2011, p. 17).

CHAPTER 3

The Causes and Stages of Alcohol Abuse: From Initiation to Alcohol Dependence

Abstract Living conditions and alcohol abuse, and the phases from initiation to alcohol abuse through which users of alcohol may move, have been described. Phases move in sequence from non-use to use, misuse, abuse and finally to dependence; each phase requires separate treatment which have been described. Lifestyle, personal characteristics and behaviour may constitute risk factors that may contribute to the developing of diseases resulting from the abuse of alcohol. As the consumption of alcohol becomes chronic, it becomes a habitual social activity and eventually the abuser of alcohol becomes dependent on this substance. The user then may develop various cognitive and physical impairments which can result in acute and chronic diseases and social problems.

Keywords Living conditions and alcohol abuse · Suicide · Pathways · Initiation · Alcohol dependence · Intervention · Prevention · Stages of alcohol use · Chronic and acute diseases · Patterns of alcohol use

1 Introduction

This chapter has been divided into two sections: (a) living conditions and alcohol abuse and (b) the pathways from initiation to alcohol abuse. In the first section, living conditions and lifestyles are seen as important risk factors. The association between unemployment, suicide and alcohol abuse has also been explained.

J. Joshua, *The Economics of Addictive Behaviours Volume II*,
DOI 10.1007/978-3-319-54425-0_3

The stages through which abusers of alcohol may move have been explained in the second section.

Living Conditions and Alcohol Abuse

Various conditions may contribute towards the abuse of alcohol, such as living environment, quality of life, socio-demographics and sociocultural origin (see Fig. 3.1). Lifestyle, personal characteristics and behaviour may constitute risk factors that may contribute to the developing of diseases resulting from the abuse of alcohol. In New Zealand, 83% of those living in the most affluent areas were less likely to have consumed alcohol over the past 12 months than those living in deprived areas (70%), but those living in the most deprived areas were twice as likely to have hazardous drinking patterns as compared with those living in the least deprived areas (NZMA, 2015, p. 07).

Popovici and French (2013) investigated the relationship between changes in an individual's status of employment and the consumption of alcohol. They found a positive relationship between unemployment and the drinking of alcohol. Popovici and French (2013) found that unemployed men had a 31.6% higher change of being diagnosed with alcohol dependence or alcohol abuse (p. 457), while unemployed women had a 67.4% greater chance of being diagnosed with alcohol abuse or dependence (p. 457) over the last 12 months. They argued that job losses lead to higher alcohol abuse and dependence because of greater stress and

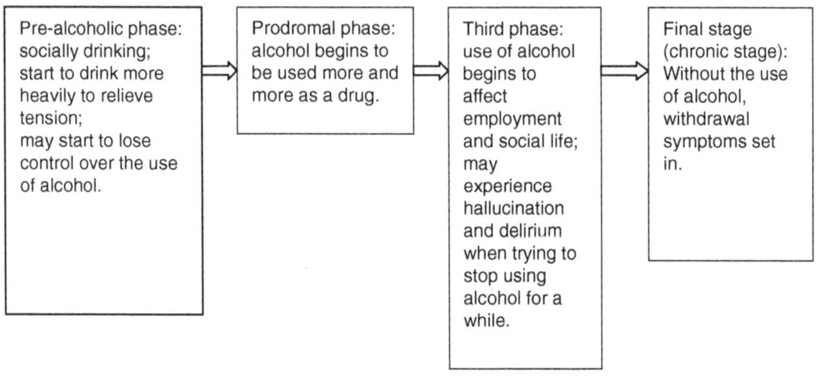

Fig. 3.1 The four different phase of alcohol use

anticipated that the current widespread unemployment as a result of the "current world-wide recession may be generating an ancillary public health crisis that will become more transparent during the coming years" (p. 462). The effect of a declining economy on various indicators of health in the United States, including unemployment, has been well documented by Catalano et al. (2011).

The abuse of alcohol has a negative effect on employment as well as earnings (Mullahy and Sindlar, 1996; Johansson et al., 2007; MacDonald and Shields, 2004; and Terza, 2002). However, there is also a reciprocal relationship between alcohol consumption and unemployment. Unemployment causes stress and anxiety which may cause the consumption of alcohol to increase. Unemployment can lead towards the abuse of alcohol. Stuckler et al. (2009) found that an increase of 3.0% in the rate of unemployment led to an increase in mortality caused by the abuse of alcohol by 28.0% and 4.45% increase in the rate of suicide for those less than 65 years of age. However, the level of alcohol consumed during times of unemployment is less, but the drinking pattern becomes more risky (Dee, 2001).

Walsh and Walsh (2011) found that the consumption of alcohol and the rate of unemployment had a significant influence on the rate of suicide among younger Irish males between the late 1980s and the end of the century. Caces and Hartford (1998) found for the period 1934–1987 in the United States that the consumption of alcohol was related to the rate of suicide when the rate of unemployment was included in the model, whereby it can be argued that unemployment was the cause and the abuse of alcohol may be seen as the facilitator. Walsh and Walsh (2011) also pointed out that in Ireland, the increasing rate of suicide since 2007 may be due to a surge in the rate of unemployment; however, this was largely dampened by a decline in the consumption of alcohol.

Walsh and Walsh (2011) argued that alcohol as "a causal factor in suicide mortality is reinforced by the evidence that in the early years of this century, when unemployment was stable at a low level, the turning point in alcohol consumption coincided with a turning point in the suicide rate, especially among younger males" (pp. 43–44). However, unemployment is only one of many factors why people may decide to commit suicide. The abuse of alcohol still may only act as a facilitator in the process of committing suicide. It is the underlying factors that may drive some people towards suicide, and the same factors may drive them to abuse alcohol which then increases the rate of suicide. Rossow (1996) also found a substantial link between the consumption of alcohol and suicide which increases with intoxication. Helliwell (2004) in an economic literature survey found that a decline in income and social capital due to recessions also causes an increase in the suicide rates.

However, various restrictive alcohol policies have been successful in reducing the detrimental effects of alcohol abuse. The success of restrictive alcohol policies has been illustrated by "the reduction in the per capita consumption of alcohol from 13.3 to 6.7 litres between 1984 and 1986" (p. 5) during the anti-alcohol campaign; at the same time, there was "a decrease in the number of BAC-positive suicide rates from 15.4 to 7.0 per 100,000 of residents" (Razvodovsky, 2011, p. 5). Ramstedt (2001b) also found that for the period between 1950 and 1995, when there was an increase in the drinking population in 14 European Union countries, the rates of suicides increased by 8.6% in northern Europe for each litre of alcohol for men and 11.4% for women. However, the increase in the suicide rate was substantially less in southern Europe and central Europe.

The Pathways from Initiation to Alcohol Dependence

There are multiple reasons why users of alcohol begin to use alcohol in excess; but regardless of the initial cause, users may go through various phases. Jellinek (1952) defined four phases through which alcoholics pass as they move towards addiction. During the pre-alcoholic phase, individuals drink socially and may start to drink more heavily to relieve tension and may start to lose control over the use of alcohol. During the prodromal phase, alcohol begins to be used more and more as a drug rather than as a beverage. The third phase is regarded by Jellinek (1952) as crucial because the use of alcohol during this phase affects employment and social life. The users in this phase may experience hallucination and delirium when they try to stop consuming alcohol; however, they are still able to abstain from the use of alcohol for a while but with another drink, Jellinek (1952) argued, the cycle of alcohol abuse starts again. During the final stage, the chronic stage, the consumption of alcohol is on a continuing basis and without the use of alcohol withdrawal symptoms will set in.

The four different phases of drug use require each a separate appropriate method of intervention. Phases move in sequence from non-use to use, misuse, abuse and finally to dependence. Prevention is used when subjects are not taking any drugs. At the level of infrequent use of drugs, generally no treatment is required but many abusers of drugs were also once at this stage so that many infrequent users will graduate to the level of full drug users. At the stage of misuse, early intervention is required. At the stage of abuse, intervention, often in the form of in- or outpatient treatment, is required. During the stage of dependence, detoxification and in- or outpatient treatment is required. The four phases are illustrated in Fig. 3.1.

However, Fig. 3.2 shows the pathways from a different aspect, that is, from initiation to chronic and acute diseases, where the pathways are illustrated by three phases together with the possible consequences of drug use, that is, acute and chronic social problems and acute and chronic diseases. Figure 3.2 is also shown in volume I in this series of The Economics of Addictive Behaviour as it illustrates the pathways from initiation to chronic and acute diseases and so that this figure can be related to all drugs.

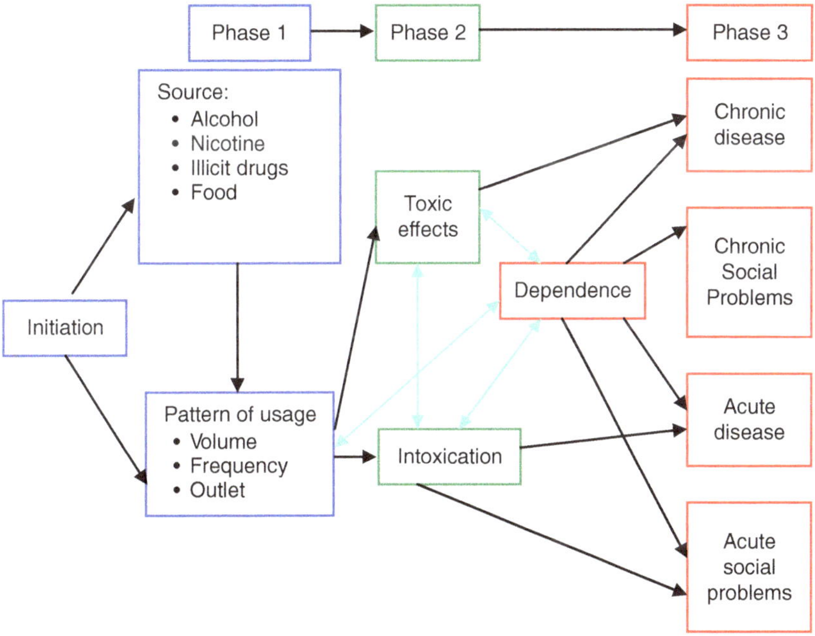

Fig. 3.2 The pathways from initiation to chronic and acute diseases

Although more attention is being paid to acute problems, such as driving under the influence, violence and public disturbance, than to the chronic diseases that may result from the abuse of alcohol, such as various forms of cancers, for example, cancer of the prostate, pancreas, colon, rectum, liver, breast, pancreatic cancer, and cancers of the mouth, nasopharynx, oropharynx and other pharynx, laryngeal cancer, and oesophageal. The risk multiplies with the number of drinks (Rehm and Shield, 2013; Nelson et al., 2013).

In most situations, consumers of alcohol have been initiated into the use of alcohol by peers or role models. Adolescents and adults often imitate the behaviour of other people; for example, there are not many movies in which people do not smoke, drink alcohol or eat something or other so that it is perceived as a normal social activity; when it is then followed as a role model, it may eventually develop into a bandwagon effect.

The early initiation to the use of any forms of drugs is a risk factor for the development of substance use disorder, lower educational performance and other detrimental effects in their future. The harmful use and eventual abuse of drugs, such as nicotine, alcohol and illicit drugs, are potential precursors for drug dependence. The consumption of alcohol amongst adolescents between the ages of 14 and 16 may be followed by truancy a year later and truancy may also lead to the consumption of alcohol. Engberg and Morral (2006) found that a reduction in drug use by adolescents is associated with better school attendance and therefore has also a positive effect on economic and social benefits which are also associated with a better school attendance.

Early initiation to illicit drugs and alcohol use is associated with increased dependence on a particular drug and treatment admission in later life. Bandura (1986) argued that the main reasons why adolescents start to use alcohol are social and cultural factors; they learn by watching others and imitate what they perceive to be culturally appropriate behaviour, to be part of the "crowd". Cultural practices appear in habits of eating or in the consumption of alcohol in order to seek an identity in social gatherings, whereby "taste classifies, and it classifies the classifier. Social subjects, classified by their classifications, distinguish themselves by the distinctions they made" (Bourdieu, 1984, p. 6), and so find their own identity.

Individuals may increase their consumption of alcohol by processes of operant conditioning whereby users of alcohol continue their use through reinforcement which may be positive or negative. They experience positive reinforcement when they like the taste which they have acquired or find the use of alcohol as a "social lubricator" in social gatherings. On the other hand, they may experience negative reinforcement when they use alcohol to reduce stress; generally, the higher the stress they experience, the more alcohol they consume (Wills, 1986).

As the consumption of alcohol becomes chronic, it becomes a habitual social activity and eventually the abuser of alcohol becomes dependent on this substance. The user then develops eventually various cognitive and physical impairments. It is the drinking pattern, that is, the frequency of alcohol consumption and the outlet or the occasion and the quantity consumed which are most important and which determines the effect of the consumption of alcohol. The occasion may be a dinner which makes it less harmful then when alcohol is consumed without food, or especially when consumers use alcohol alone in social isolation. The consumption of alcohol may then lead to a great number of preventable diseases (see Fig. 3.2).

The harm caused through the abuse of alcohol is mainly caused by two factors, that is, the volume of alcohol and the pattern of drinking alcohol. The quality of alcohol may also play an important role in certain situations as in the case of unrecorded consumption, that is, home produced alcoholic beverages (Rehm et al., 2003).

Patterns of alcohol use refer to the drinking behaviour, such as where and when drinking takes place, number of episodes and heavy drinking, types of alcoholic beverages consumed and the social environment in which drinking occurs. The pattern of drinking alcohol may greatly influence the detrimental effects, for example, while drinking with a meal causes less harm or none at all, than when people going on a binge (see Stranges et al., 2004). The detrimental effects of alcohol abuse are caused by the frequency and volume of alcohol consumed during a person's lifetime, as well as the quantity of alcohol during a drinking session, whereby the frequency and volume of episodic heavy drinking will especially increase the risk of cardiovascular diseases and injuries (Anderson, 2012, p. 5).

Alcohol is an addictive drug and an immunosuppressant so that the risk of communicable diseases increases. It may result in cancer of the oral cavity, pharynx, liver, colon, rectum and the breast. The risk for causing such cancers increases with the quantity of alcohol consumption (Rehm et al., 2010a). The abuse of alcohol is a major cause of various non-communicable diseases, such as various forms of cancers, cardiovascular diseases and liver cirrhoses. It is also a cause of various communicable diseases, such as tuberculosis and HIV/AIDS. It is a cause of intentional and unintentional injuries. Alcohol contributes about 60 different diseases and disorders, such as cardiovascular diseases, various forms of cancers, such as lung cancer, gastrointestinal conditions, skeletal and muscular diseases (see Anderson and Baumberg, 2006). Eight years later, the World Health Organization (2014) report on alcohol and health made the point that alcohol abuse contributes to more than 200 diseases. The consumption worldwide in 2010 was 6.2 l/year of pure alcohol or 13.5 g /day for each person of 15 years of age or over (World Health Organization, 2014, p. 29).

The main effect which contributes to the detrimental effects of the consumption of alcohol is the toxic effect which causes damage to body organs and tissues. Alcohol like any other drug is a toxic substance, although the physical and psychological effects of the toxic substances differ between the different drugs. The other main effect is intoxication which causes acute health effects mainly through cognitive coordination affect on behaviour. The abuse of alcohol also leads to dependence so that the abuser's self-control becomes impaired. The pattern of usage in terms of volume, frequency and outlet which results in heavy drinking leads to numerous chronic diseases such as ailments of the liver, cancers and cardiovascular disorders. Drinking patterns that increase the blood alcohol levels lead to acute intoxication and thus may result in violence, accidents and injuries (see Fig. 3.2).

Alcohol has acute and chronic effects. Acute effects lead to, for example, accidents and violence because of cognitive impairment whereas chronic effects cause various diseases, such as cirrhosis of the liver. Young adolescents lose more years of life, productivity and have a lower quality of life because of acute alcohol problems, whereas older consumers of alcohol experience detrimental effect as a result of chronic diseases (see Chikritzha et al., 2001).

The processes of the three separate phases from initiation to chronic and acute diseases that consumers of alcohol may go through when they abuse alcohol for a longer time, as outlined in Fig. 3.2, will be discussed throughout the book.

CHAPTER 4

The Consequences of Alcohol Abuse

Abstract Psychoactive substances are addictive, and the behavioural and biological mechanisms of addiction are discussed together with the physiological, psychosocial and pharmacological consequences of alcohol abuse. The processes of alcohol abuse and alcohol dependence, together with alcohol as a means of self-medication, are described in details. This chapter will highlight the correlation between the consumption of beer, wine and spirits, whereby beer and spirits are the most correlated. Abusers of alcohol may eventually also move on to other drugs. The consumption of marijuana is closely related to the consumption of tobacco as well as alcohol. Marijuana and alcoholic beverages contain similar intoxicating properties and so serve similar wants and so may be used as substitutes. Prohibition has various unintended harmful consequences.

Keywords Physiological effects · Psychosocial effects · Pharmacological effects · Processes of alcohol abuse and dependence · Alcoholism · Anxiolytic use of alcohol

1 Introduction

This chapter discusses the consequences of alcohol abuse and is separated into three sections: (a) the physiological effects of alcohol abuse, (b) the psychosocial effects of alcohol abuse and (c) the processes of alcohol abuse and alcohol dependence.

J. Joshua, *The Economics of Addictive Behaviours Volume II*,
DOI 10.1007/978-3-319-54425-0_4

The clinical criteria of alcohol abuse involve various specific diagnostic criteria; however, the abuse of alcohol may go beyond the clinical criteria; for example, car accidents and road fatalities may be the consequence of a single episode of driving under the influence; however, it would not meet the clinical definition of alcohol abuse but may cause greater social costs resulting from the abuse of alcohol than caused by people who meet the criteria of alcohol abuse.

The Physiological Effect of Alcohol Abuse

Alcohol has various characteristics which causes detrimental effects on people's health. Alcohol causes dependence through neuro-adaptation and its reinforcing properties. As an immunosuppressant, it increases the risk of communicable diseases, such as tuberculosis. Alcohol is also neurotoxic and thus causes structural hippocampal changes during adolescents. Alcohol is also a teratogen which has a detrimental effect on the foetus, such as cognitive deficiencies. Alcohol has been classified amongst asbestos and formaldehyde as a group 1 carcinogen by the World Health Organization's International Agency for Research on Cancer since 1988. As a carcinogen, alcohol increases the risk of various cancers, such as of the pharynx, oesophagus, stomach, colon, rectum and breast (Anderson et al., 2009, pp. 2234–2236). Alcohol is metabolized in the liver through various stages; it is first converted into acetaldehyde and then into acetate. Approximately 75% of acetate moves to other issues where oxidation to carbon dioxide and water is completed.

The abuse of alcohol has been associated with over 60 diseases (Gutjahr et al., 2001; Room et al., 2005). The list of diseases associated with the excessive use of alcohol has now been extended to over 200 diseases, conditions and injuries as listed in the International Classification of Diseases, revision 10 (ICD-10). Chronic excessive consumption of alcohol can cause an increase in the blood pressure and may cause various chronic diseases, such as cardiovascular and liver diseases, especially liver cirrhosis, various types of cancers, especially of the liver, myopathy, kidney diseases and pancreatitis. Rehm et al. (2003) have illustrated how chronic heavy drinking may cause death resulting from organ damage, such as liver cirrhosis. The excess consumption of alcohol may cause coronary heart disease, supraventricular cardiac dysrhythmias, tuberculosis, pancreatitis, breast cancer, damages the endocrine glands, alcoholic gastritis, spontaneous abortion, epilepsy and cancer of oesophagus.

Alcohol abuse has a detrimental effect on hypertensive diseases (Taylor et al., 2009), haemorrhagic stroke (Patra et al., 2010) and atrial fibrillation (Samokhvalov et al., 2010). Long-term heavy drinking is a considerable risky factor for depression and anxiety disorders. The excessive consumption of alcohol can lead towards deficiencies in thiamine (vitamin B) and folate. Deficiency of thiamine may result in tiny brain haemorrhages and damage brain cells and may cause cortical atrophy and mental illness.

Thiamine deficiency can result in Korsakoff-Wernicke syndromes which produce short-term memory loss, and the abuse of alcohol may also cause cerebral dementia. The Korsakoff-Wernicke disease is a metabolic disorder of the central nervous system resulting from a thiamine deficiency (vitamin B) causing a severe loss of memory. The syndrome is usually progressive; even though it may be treated with considerable doses of vitamin B, it cannot be reversed; although there may be some recovery. Thus, alcoholism can also cause Korsakoff's syndrome which is an amnesic syndrome caused by a degeneration of the dorsomedial thalamic nucleus resulting from chronic alcoholism.

The intake of inappropriate nutrition and the consumption of ethanol can induce osteopenia which implies a low bone density and may develop into osteoporosis. The rate of suicide also increases with an increase in alcohol, while injuries are the most common consequence of alcohol consumption, and the number of motor vehicle accidents increases with an increase in the consumption of alcohol as well.

The excessive drinking of alcohol during pregnancy is also detrimental to the foetus and may lead to foetal spectrum disorder causing various mental and physical defects which consists of a wide range of physical cognitive and behavioural impairments, and it is the major preventable cause of developmental disabilities. However, there is no safe level of alcohol consumption during any stage of pregnancy. If pregnant women consume alcohol heavily, it may lead towards foetal alcohol syndrome which may cause cranial, facial and limb anomalies; and it can also retard the growth of the foetus and may cause mental retardation and cognitive disabilities, low body weight and abnormal appearance. However, von Hinke Kessler Scholder et al. (2014) showed that "low-to-moderate alcohol exposure *in utero* may have similar negative effects on the foetus that may be carried into childhood and adolescence" (p. 662). Prenatal alcohol exposure may interfere with foetal development and thus may cause behavioural problems later in life (see Famy et al., 1998).

Mattson et al. (1998, (12); pp. 146–153) showed that children who have been exposed to foetal alcohol syndrome have a considerable lower intelligence quotient and therefore reduces their capability to learn and to acquire skills and also decreases their quality of life. However, adults who also suffer from foetal alcohol syndrome often experience substantial mental illness, such as depression, psychotic disorders and drug dependence.

Cooper (1987) stated that pregnant women who consume two to four drinks per day provide a health hazard for their infant, such as being born with low birth weight, while the consumption of more than four drinks may cause foetal alcohol syndrome which may lead to cognitive and physical defects. With every increase in the consumption of alcohol, the chances of foetal alcohol syndrome increase, for example, Sarafino (1990, p. 237) stated that for the general population, the incidence rate is 0.4 per 1,000 births but can be as high as 690 per 1,000 births.

Worldwide, 5.9% of all deaths are attributable to the consumption of alcohol; in comparison, HIV/AIDS causes 2.8%, violence 0.9% and tuberculosis causes 1.7%. The consumption of alcohol contributes 5.1% to global diseases and injuries (World Health Organization, 2014, p. 46). However, Anderson and Baumberg (2006) made the point that the contribution of alcohol towards mortality may be understated; for example, citing a study of 12 cities in 10 countries by Puffer and Griffith (1967) which revealed that the cases of liver cirrhosis related to alcohol consumption increased by 135% after investigation (pp. 134–5). Likewise, Ramsteadt (2003) found that 65% of recorded deaths from non-alcoholic cirrhosis of the liver were actually due to the consumption of alcohol.

Kerr et al. (2000) found the overall level of drinking and consumption of spirits to be associated with liver cirrhoses in Australia, Canada, New Zealand, United Kingdom and the USA. Ramstedt (2001a) in a study on 14 European countries and Mills (2007) found a significant effect of the consumption of alcohol on mortality due to cirrhosis in the United Kingdom. The probability of liver cirrhosis increases with a pattern of heavy drinking over a number of years, whereby women are at greater risk; however, "almost ninety per cent of the cirrhosis mortality cases are found in the male population" (Bentzen and Smith, 2010, p. 4).

Heavy drinkers may consume cheaper alcohol beverages, for example beer; hence, beer may have a considerable effect on liver cirrhosis; even though beer has a lower content of alcohol, but it is consumed in greater quantity. Bentzen and Smith (2010) found that beer, wine and spirits as well as the level of alcohol consumption contribute to the mortality due to liver cirrhosis. The consumption of beer, wine and spirits is correlated, whereby beer and spirits are the most correlated. Bentzen and Smith (2010) found that beer, spirits and wine all have an effect on liver cirrhoses, but beer has the strongest effect; in contrast to Mills's (2007) study, the consumption of wine is highly correlated to liver cirrhosis, whereas Kerr et al. (2000) found spirits to produce the greatest detrimental effect on liver cirrhosis; on the other hand, Becker et al. (2002) found wine to be a lesser contributor to liver cirrhosis. However, as Bentzen and Smith (2010) made the point, it is not so much the drink per se which contributes to detrimental health effects, but rather the actual content of alcohol. Hence, many of the studies are inconclusive and often contradict each other regarding the detrimental effects on drinkers' health of the types of alcoholic drinks.

The consumption of alcohol increases the probability of haemorrhagic stroke (Reynolds et al., 2003). On the other hand, the consumption of alcohol has been found by some studies, such as by Sacco et al. (1999), that at a low level of consumption of alcohol, it reduces the probability of an ischemic stroke. However, Mazzaglia et al. (2001) combining numerous studies did not find any evidence that the low consumption of alcohol provides any protection against an ischemic stroke.

Irving et al. (2009) found that the risk of pancreatitis sharply increased with an increase in the consumption of alcohol. Individuals consuming 3.6 g of alcohol daily, or about three standard drinks, had 1.2 times the risk compared with non-drinkers, "whereas, those with a daily alcohol intake of 9.6 grams, or eight standard drinks, had a four-fold increased risk of pancreatic" (p. 390). They found that "the threshold of alcohol associated with the risk of pancreatitis was about 4 drinks daily" (p. 390).

There is generally a dose–response relationship; for example, not only does the abuse of alcohol contribute to the development of cancer, but the greater the consumption of alcohol, the greater will be the risk of developing cancer (Shield et al., 2013), as in the case of gastrointestinal diseases, such as liver cirrhosis (Rehm et al., 2010b) and pancreatic (acute and chronic) (Irving et al., 2009).

The excess consumption of alcohol suppresses the immune system so that consumers of alcohol are more susceptible to infectious diseases. There is a curvilinear relationship between the consumption of alcohol and diabetes; that is, while it is thought to have a protective effect at low level of consumption, there is an increased risk with the volume of alcohol consumed; in this case, there could be a U-shape relationship between alcohol consumption and mortality in some diseases.

Rehm (2011) stated that two standard drinks, that is, 28 g of pure alcohol per day, have the greatest protective effect, while the net detrimental effect begins at about four standard drinks per day (p. 138). On the other hand, the effect of alcohol consumption on hypertension has a linear relationship; that is, the higher the dose, the greater the risk with an increase in consumption. In the case of ischemic heart disease, the association with the consumption of alcohol follows a J-shaped curve; that is, regular light drinking is thought to be protective which however can be nullified through heavy drinking occasions (Rehm, 2011).

However, epidemiological studies may have overestimated the benefits of low alcohol consumption on ischemic heart disease; for example, those who consume alcohol at a low rate usually also have a healthier lifestyle than heavy drinkers, and some who abstain from any consumption of alcohol may do so because they have some adverse health problems (Chikritzhs et al., 2009).

Schaeffer and Ritz (2012) described the relationship between consumers of alcohol and the adverse effects as being Janus-faced. Excessive consumption of alcohol has adverse effects on kidney, whereas moderate alcohol consumption is associated with less cardiovascular and renal risk.

The Psychosocial Effects of Alcohol Abuse

Alcoholic beverages contain ethyl alcohol which is a psychoactive ingredient and as such is classified as a drug. Substance abuse for most people concerns the abuse of illicit drugs; however, legal drugs such as alcohol and nicotine may do greater harm than some illicit drugs. Nutt et al. (2007) made the point that the use of alcohol and smoking are classified as being more harmful than a class A drug, for example LSD, and argued that alcohol could be classified as a class A drug and smoking could be classified under class B. Psychoactive substances are highly addictive, and the behavioural and physiological characteristics of nicotine, alcohol and illicit drugs are similar so that there is a considerable overlap between the population of users and abusers of such drugs (see Booth et al., 2009).

Faith et al. (2009) made the point that most psychological disability is caused through the abuse of alcohol which often is related to various interpersonal, intrapersonal and occupational difficulties. Relationship between alcohol abuse and intimate partner violence has been well researched and documented (Averett and Wang, 2016). Intimate partner violence is the most common type of violence against women and it is more common than rape and exceeds the violence perpetrated by stranger (World Health Organization, 2005).

The abuse of alcohol may lead to a lower moral responsibility. The availability of alcohol can be expected to increase intimate violence in much the same way as it increases any other crime which thought to increase with the abuse of alcohol. This has been confirmed in the case of Australia by Livingston (2010). As the consumption of alcoholic beverages increases so do the adverse consequences of alcohol abuse. However, Averett and Wang (2016) found that alcohol is likely to be only a correlate rather than a cause of intimate partner violence between young adult males and their intimate partner.

Familial difficulties and economic difficulties will foster instability within the family which may hamper the development of stable personality which is less likely to submit to the temptation of alcohol abuse. A generational transmission of alcohol abuse may also include genetic causes. The difficulties that students experience increase when alcohol abuse stretches within two or more generations. The problems for young adolescents also intensify when both parents were involved in alcohol abuse. Thus, prior alcohol abuse within a family increases the probability for young adolescents from such families also to enter various stages of alcohol abuse. Alcohol abuse preventions have to take into account the generational history of alcohol abuse within the family (see Berkowitz and Perkins, 1987; Perkins and Berkowitz, 1991). Perkins and Berkowitz found that there was a considerable generational transmission of alcohol abuse which confirms previous research by Cotton (1979).

Familial, economic, emotional and economic difficulties will foster instability within the family which may hamper the development of stable personality which is less likely to submit to the temptation of alcohol abuse. A generational transmission of alcohol abuse may also include genetic components. Students will face various difficulties when alcohol abuse stretches within a family over two generations. The problem for young adolescents also intensifies when both parents are involved in alcohol abuse. Thus, prior alcohol abuse within a family increases the probability for adolescents coming from such families also to enter various stages of alcohol abuse. Alcohol abuse preventions have to take into account the generational history of alcohol abuse (see Berkowitz and Perkins, 1987).

The way how parents consume alcohol also has an effect on how their children may consume alcohol and drugs later. However, parental influence is only one of the environmental factors which serves as a role model and thereby influences the attitudes towards alcohol abuse and the taking of drugs. The integration of drug education into the alcohol curriculum has been tried with the aim of reducing drug abuse but has largely failed as it was based on the mistaken assumption that providing factual information would deter adolescents from abusing drugs (Gorsuch and Butler, 1976). Drug abusers perceive various unfulfilled needs which they try to meet through the abuse of drugs which they assume may be fulfilled through the use of drugs, which may be fulfilled initially through experimentation Goodman (1970).

Goodman (1970) argued that the inability to cope is a major motive for predependency which is caused through the psychic pain, with which individuals are unable to cope so that drug abuse is used as a way of coping with such psychic pain and the inability to cope. The expected outcome of drug abuse is the reduction in discomfort and so may lead towards drug abuse. The consumption of alcohol and drugs is seen as a way to relieve stress, tension and anxiety and depression. However, various alcohol and drug abusers need a considerable amount of the drug before they experience a decline in stress. However, intoxication will not reduce an adolescents' psychic pain and indeed often increases such pain. Bandura (1977) argued that alcohol is regarded as especially functional as it anaesthetizes any psychic pain. The use of alcohol often provides individuals with accuses for committing violent acts. Graham and Gross (1975) found that adolescent drug abusers were inclined to be disdainful towards rules and were inclined to act to satisfy their short-term gratifications and had a relatively low impulse control. There is often a general denial during the earlier stages of alcohol abuse. It may also be argued that knowledge of the consequences of alcohol abuse is insufficient to deter abuser from the abuse of alcohol. Moskowitz (1989) argued that it may be able to reinforce other social marketing messages. Hence, most abusers also underestimate their abuse of alcohol.

Alcohol is a contributor to psychiatric morbidity, such as depression and suicide (Borges and Loera, 2010). Comorbid alcohol abuse frequently occurs in schizophrenia (Arndt et al., 1992), bipolar disorder (Goldstein et al., 2006). The rates of suicides are strongly influenced by the abuse of alcohol when it occurs in countries which have a drinking culture of heavy drinking episodes. Walsh and Walsh (2011) found that the consumption of alcohol and the rate of unemployment had a significant influence on the rate of suicide among younger Irish males between the late 1980s and the end of the century. Caces and Hartford (1998) found, for the period

1934–1987 in the United States, that the consumption of alcohol was related to the rate of suicide when the rate of unemployment was included in the model, whereby it can be argued that unemployment was the cause and the abuse of alcohol may be seen as the facilitator. Walsh and Walsh (2011) also pointed out that in Ireland, the increasing rate of suicide since 2007 may be due to a surge in the rate of unemployment; however, this was largely dampened by a decline in the consumption of alcohol.

Walsh and Walsh (2011) argued that alcohol as "a causal factor in suicide mortality is reinforced by the evidence that in the early years of this century, when unemployment was stable at a low level, the turning point in alcohol consumption coincided with a turning point in the suicide rate, especially among younger males" (pp. 43–44). However, there are other factors involved besides unemployment why people may decide to commit suicide; hence, alcohol still only acts as a facilitator in the process of committing suicide. It is the underlying factors that may drive some people towards suicide and the same factors may drive them to abuse alcohol which then increases the rate of suicide. Helliwell (2004) also found in an economic literature survey that a decline in income and social capital due to recessions causes an increase in the suicide rates.

Bedford et al. (2006) found in various coroners' reports in Ireland in 2000–2001 on suicide high blood alcohol concentrations in young males. However, this does not imply necessarily a direct link between the consumption of alcohol and suicide. A happy person who is intoxicated does generally not commit suicide; instead, there is always another intervening variable, such as depression, which may cause a person to think about committing suicide. The consumption of alcohol may merely reduce the inhibition to commit suicide; that is, alcohol may help to facilitate suicide but it is not the initial cause. Hence, it may be depression or some other factors which leads a depressed person to abuse alcohol which may then lead to suicide.

Furthermore, there is a difference between suicide which is "alcohol-related", the term which is used by Anderson and Baumberg (2006), and suicide which is "alcohol-attributable", the term used by Martin et al. (2010). Hence, committing suicide because of a depressed state of mind may be related to alcohol abuse when the person committing suicide was under the influence of alcohol, but such a suicide was caused by the person's depression; that is, it was attributable to depression, even though it may be alcohol related, but it may not be attributable to alcohol per se, but rather to depression. Similarly, family violence is often attributed to alcohol; however, the consumption of alcohol is unlikely to make a person violent unless the perpetrator has a violent personality in the first place which may be unleashed through the abuse of alcohol, as the abuse of alcohol may lead to a person's inability to exercise self-control.

Various problems which may lead individuals to abuse alcohol may also cause individuals to commit suicide (Brainerd, 2001). Brainerd (2001) amongst others found a positive significant effect of the consumption of alcohol and the rate of suicide during the economic reform period of the Soviet Union during the 1990s. Razvodovsky (2011) found that an increase in the consumption of alcohol by 1 l has increased the rate of suicide by 8.8% and concluded that a more restrictive alcohol policy may be an effective way to reduce the rate of suicide. The acute and chronic abuses of alcohol are both involved in suicidal behaviour (Norström, 1995). Acute alcohol abuse impairs individuals' cognitive functioning which prevents effective coping skills to be used (Hufford, 2001; Lester, 1998).

Alcohol-related accidents that involve cars are also a major contributor to death and resulting disabilities. Over 50% of fatalities in car accidents involved drivers who had alcohol in their blood. Twenty-five per cent of hospitalized individuals were at least partly due to alcohol (Rosenhan and Seligman, 1984, p. 424). The number of users of alcohol is related to its availability or number of outlets. As the legal drinking age was lowered in many of the states in the United States, traffic accidents and fatalities of 18 and 19-year olds increased between 20% and 50% (Rosenhan and Seligman, 1984, p. 424). Consequently, as some states have again raised the legal drinking age, traffic accidents amongst this age group declined by about 20% (Rosenhan and Seligman, 1984, p. 424). Rosenhan and Seligman (1984) made the point that alcohol as the "body drug" had a far more detrimental effect during the mid-1980s than marijuana the "mind drug". Amongst young drivers with blood alcohol content of alcohol, the association between alcohol abuse and car accidents and violent crimes is similar (Roizen, 1993).

Alcohol affects the central nervous system like other depressant drugs causing disinhibition and relaxation at low dosage, as higher dosage will impair judgment and impair coordination. Hence, adverse social consequences are often associated with excessive alcohol consumption. Episodes of alcohol intoxication cause death from overdose or from injury resulting from the violence or from accidents (Hingson and Winter, 2003). The causal relationship between alcohol abuse and aggressive behaviour has been established in various studies. A causal link between aggression and intoxication has been suggested through epidemiological studies (Collins and Schlenger, 1988; Wiley and Weisner, 1995) and biological mechanisms which relate the consumption of alcohol to aggressive behaviours has also been confirmed (Peterson et al., 1990; Sayette et al., 1993).

Furthermore, the pharmacological effects of alcohol increase the probability of aggressive behaviour (Room et al., 2005), and more crime is committed under the influence of alcohol (Parry and Dewing, 2006). There is a strong relationship between the consumption of alcohol and the rate of crime; according to the Bureau of Justice Statistics (1998), one-third of convicted offenders in 1996 were influenced by alcohol at the time of their offence. The taking of drugs in any form is often associated with social decline, that is, it is associated with a declining economy, criminality and escapism which may cause the social and economic hardship of individuals to increase and thereby have a detrimental effect on people's health.

The Processes of Alcohol Abuse and Dependence

Before alcohol abusers become alcohol dependent, they move through different phases from initiation towards alcohol dependence. During each phase, alcohol abusers require different types of intervention. As alcohol abuser moves through the different phases, they may develop various acute and chronic diseases and acute and chronic social problems (see Fig. 3.2: the pathways from initiation to chronic and acute diseases). Alcohol is now associated with over 200 diseases, conditions and injuries. Similar to illicit drugs, alcohol is also being used as a means of self-medication.

The American Psychiatric Association (1994) uses the following criteria to define alcohol dependence as described in *The Diagnostic Statistical Manual* (DSM-IV). It classifies alcohol dependence as a maladaptive pattern of the use of alcohol which caused distress or impairment of bodily or cognitive functions over the last 12 months in three or more of the following seven criteria: first, gain tolerance which requires a greater amount of alcohol to achieve intoxication or a diminishing effect of the same amount of alcohol; second, existence and withdrawal of syndrome so that alcohol is taken to either avoid or to relieve such symptoms; third, more alcohol is consumed over a longer period than is anticipated; fourth, unsuccessful attempts to reduce the intake of alcohol; fifth, a considerable time is used to satisfy the urge for alcohol, that is, obtaining it, consuming it and recovering from its use; sixth, other activities are being replaced with the activities involved in consuming alcohol; and seventh, the use of alcohol continues despite being aware of the physical or psychological damage that it will cause. According to DSM-IV, dependence is a cluster of cognitive, behavioural and physiologic symptoms.

Alcohol dependence is defined in the Diagnostic and Statistical Manual of Mental Disorders (DSM-IV). Individuals who experience an inability to exercise control over their consumption of alcohol, experience withdrawal symptoms and experience high tolerance so that they feel a need to increase their intake of alcohol.

In the DSM-V, alcohol abuse is combined with alcohol dependence and together is referred to as alcohol use disorder which includes a graded scale from moderate to severe. In the case of adolescents, a diagnosis that satisfies two or three criteria would have been regarded as alcohol abuse, while four or more criteria imply alcohol dependence under DSM-IV.

The American Psychiatric Association used to make the distinction between alcohol abuse and alcohol dependence in the *Diagnostic and Statistical Manual of Mental Disorders* (*DSM-IV*); in both cases, there is a lack of control and withdrawal symptoms are often relieved or avoided by the further consumption of alcohol. However, the American Psychiatric Association (2013) has removed in DSM-V the distinction between "abuse" and "dependence" in the case of substance abuse and alcohol abuse so that the revised DSM-V does not use the terms "alcohol abuse" and "alcohol dependence" and instead replaced them with "alcohol use disorder". This new term classifies problem drinkers as those with at least two out of 11 symptoms, such as alcohol cravings and frequent hangovers. Abuse and dependence may be seen as the same disorder on a continuum of abuse. Dependence implies that the user is physically and or psychologically dependent on a drug and experiences serious problems. A state of dependence is when a user experiences discomfort or distress when the use of a particular drug is discontinued or is severely reduced so that alcohol dependence is a combination of behavioural, cognitive and physiological phenomena.

The term "alcoholism" has been variably used, generally referring to a chronic continual drinking pattern leading frequently to intoxication. Alcoholism may be described as a chronic disease interspersed with various periods of sobriety and treatment. However, the term is rather vague (Edwards and Gross, 1976) so that the World Health Organization now favours the term of "alcohol dependence" (World Health Organization, 1980).

To optimize the benefits and to ascertain the appropriate management strategies, the economic burden of diseases has to be determined before such strategies can be appropriately implemented. According to Volpicelli (2001), alcohol dependence is one of the three most prevalent psychiatric disorders in the United States. The Center for Behavioral Health Statistics and Quality (SAMHS – Substance Abuse and Mental Health Services, 2013) stated that 9.5% of full-time workers between 18 and 64 years of age were dependent on alcohol or drugs during the last month as indicated by a survey conducted between 2008 and 2012. The heaviest abusers of alcohol were miners at 17.5% followed by construction workers with 16.6% (identified as "heavy drinkers"), while educational service and healthcare and social assistance had the lowest percentage of "heavy drinkers" at 4.7% and 4.4%, respectively. "Heavy drinking" was defined as consuming "five or more drinks" on the same occasion or within 2 hours on 5 or more days during the last 30 days. In third place were hotel and restaurant workers at 11.8%; however, they were the highest users of illicit drugs at 19.1%.

Psychoactive substances are addictive, and the behavioural and biological mechanisms of addiction are very similar for nicotine, alcohol and illicit drugs. Hence, it is not surprising that there is a considerable overlap of the population of users and abusers so that many abusers of psychoactive drugs may use more than one drug; for example, there is a considerable overlap between smokers and consumers of alcohol and users of other drugs.

Alcohol use is also due to self-medication as it may be used as an alternative to non-prescriptive drugs, such as analgesics; of course, the abuse of alcohol may contribute towards more self-medication of the symptoms caused by alcohol abuse; so that there may be a reciprocal relationship and reinforcing trend between these two processes; hence, Rayner and Chetwynd (1987) may under-estimate the influence of alcohol consumption on the purchase of non-prescribed pharmaceuticals, who believe that it is "insignificantly small" (p. 63). However, alcohol similar to tranquillizers is often used repeatedly because of their short-term effectiveness and through their repetitive use may lead towards dependence if taken over a longer period; for example, according to Bibb and Chambless (1986), approximately half of agoraphobics have resorted to the use of alcohol to control such symptoms. Even though the use of alcohol as an anxiolytic (see Fig. 4.1) may induce anxiolysis initially, alcohol becomes an anxiogenic agent as it will increase anxiety as well as

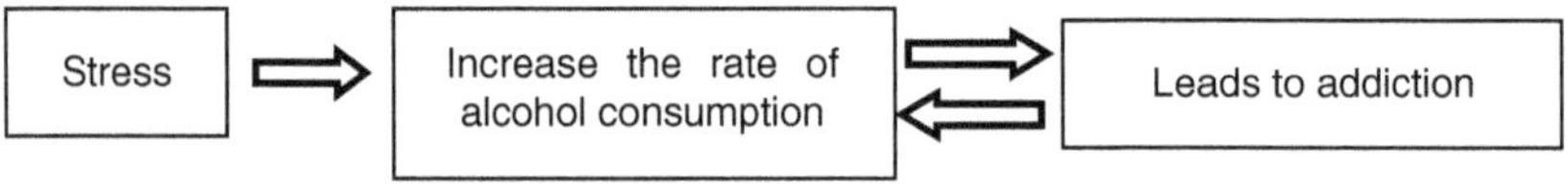

Fig. 4.1 The anxiolytic use of alcohol

depressive moods. It appears that alcohol dependence rather than the consumption of alcohol has a causal link to depression.

Alcohol consumption may lead to alcohol dependence and alcohol dependence leads to more alcohol consumption and so establishes a vicious cycle so that a deliberate effort has to be undertaken to break the cycle; otherwise, it will increase the rate of mortality. The development of alcohol dependence occurs because of biological adaptation within the brain and psychological reinforcement (World Health Organization, 2004d).

Chronic conditions, such as alcohol dependence, fluctuate over time so that conditions may improve or worsen over time regardless whether there has been any treatment; hence, a decline in the prevailing conditions of alcoholism and therefore a decline in the costs may not be related to treatment. Furthermore, the abuse of alcohol moves through stages; that is, it may move from asymptomatic heavy drinking, where abuses of alcohol are at risk to develop dependence on alcohol towards functional dependence and finally to recurrent alcohol dependence. With the habitual and chronic use of such drugs, the users develop a dependence on those drugs. The frequent use of excessive alcohol causes chronic diseases, such as cardiovascular diseases and cirrhosis of the liver and may also develop various mental health conditions, such as alcoholic psychosis, alcoholic dependence syndrome and alcohol-related dementia.

Even though depression may precede alcohol abuse and alcohol may be used by some abusers of alcohol as a means of self-medication, the consumption of alcohol increases depression as there is a considerable degree of co-morbidity when the beginning of alcohol abuse precedes depressive disorders. Indeed, after the cessation of the consumption of alcohol, depressive symptoms decrease (Brown and Schuckit, 1988; Willenbring, 1986).

The taking of alcohol and drugs increases short-term benefits which will decline long-term benefits as it declines motor performance and thereby decline physiological functions, as it declines work performance and increases staff turnover. Figure 3.1 illustrates the effect of drug abuse in the short term and in the long term. In contrast to the common belief that alcohol serves as a social lubricator, the abuse of alcohol may undermine various social relationships, such as within the family, and within the place of work; for example, Markowitz (2000) found that an increase in the price of pure alcohol as compared with a weighted average of the price of alcohol from beer, wine and liquor causes violence towards wives to decline.

Individuals who are engaged in the abuse of drugs are going through different stages and at different stages, drug abusers are motivated and influenced by different social groups so that anti-alcohol and anti-drug campaigns will have to take this into account if they are to be effective (see Bozinoff et al. 1989). The campaigns examined had greater effect on non-users rather than users in terms of evaluation of advertisement. They designed a model of six stages which has been adapted from Lettierie et al. (1980). The first stage is the non-users stage when initially the use of drugs and alcohol is not contemplated; however, the first stage was not included in the model developed by Lettieri et al. (1980). During the second stage, adolescents begin to contemplate the use of drugs. Most alcohol and drug prevention programmes are directed towards this stage. The initial use of alcohol and drugs begins in stage 3, usually having been introduced by a member of the peer group; because of the gateway effect, the novice may eventually move onto harder drugs. During stage 4, many alcohol and drug users remain light users. During stage 5, the moderate use of alcohol and drugs prevails and includes a movement away from socially acceptable light use towards heavier use. Stage 6 involves heavy use of alcohol and drugs and develops into the stage of addiction. This stage is generally not subject to marketing techniques (De Paulo et al. 1987). The movement from stage 4 to 5 and finally to stage 6 is largely caused by a perceived need.

Different categories of drinkers have different reasons for drinking alcohol. Hazardous drinkers generally have more reasons to consume alcohol than non-hazardous drinkers (Wiggins and Wiggens, 1987). Hazardous drinkers are also more likely to consume alcohol for mood changing reasons, that is, to relax. It can also be expected that hazardous drinkers are the least happy drinkers, hence their intention to resort to drinking alcohol at the same time while they are also least happy with their drinking of alcohol at a hazardous level. Capuzzi and Lecoq (1983) argued that a lack of loving care and closeness between parent and child appears to promote the stage when adolescents perceive drug use as being positive and rewarding, possibly a compensation or a lack of a warm and close relationship between the child and parents.

Abusers of alcohol may eventually move on to other drugs. The use of other drugs, especially of marijuana, has increased. Clements et al. (2010) found that the consumption of marijuana is closely related to the consumption of tobacco as well as alcohol. Marijuana and alcoholic beverages may be regarded as complements as well as a substitute. When Marijuana is mixed with tobacco products and alcohol, then marijuana may be regarded as complements. Marijuana and alcoholic beverages contain similar intoxicating properties and so serve similar wants and so may be used as substitutes. Prohibition has various unintended harmful consequences. Therefore, it may be argued that decriminalization of the abuse of illegal drugs is a most ineffective way in controlling or reducing the abuse as it increases the rate of crime, corruption, violence and the uncertain quality of the drug concerned. In some countries where the abuse of the drugs has been decriminalized, the actual demand of such drugs could be controlled to some extant through taxation policy similar to taxes placed on tobacco product and alcoholic beverages. Becker and Murphy (1988) made the point that the tax revenue gained in the case of marijuana being legalized, and the change in the demand for marijuana would depend on the own- and cross-price elasticities of marijuana, alcohol and tobacco. Hence, a change in tax revenue will depend on the demand for marijuana.

The consumption of marijuana is closely related to the consumption of tobacco as well as alcohol. Marijuana and alcoholic beverages may be regarded as complements as well as a substitute. When Marijuana is mixed with tobacco products and alcohol, then Marijuana may be regarded as complements. Marijuana and alcoholic beverages contain similar intoxicating properties and so serve similar wants and so may be used as substitutes. Prohibition has various unintended harmful consequences. Therefore, it may be argued that decriminalization of the abuse of illegal drugs is a most ineffective way in controlling or reducing the abuse as it increases the rate of crime, corruption, violence and the uncertain quality of the drug concerned. In some countries where the abuse of the drugs has been decriminalized, the actual demand of such drugs could be controlled to some extant through taxation policy similar to taxes placed on tobacco product and alcoholic beverages.

When marijuana is legalized and taxed, the marijuana price depends largely on the tax rate. However, when marijuana is legalized and not taxed, the price of marijuana would decline because producers of marijuana would not anymore incur the costs of avoiding the ban, such as avoiding the costs of being prosecuted, such as avoiding prosecution the costs of which are the costs of ion which are the costs of operating an illegal business. As under legalization of marijuana, the risk premium disappears so that the price of marijuana falls, the price of marijuana will remain unchanged when the imposed tax cancels out the effect of the disappearance/the elimination of the risk premium. When the imposed tax is less than the risk premium, the consumer price will fall (Miller and Moulton, 2014).

Legalization of dealing in marijuana and other drugs will cause the risk premium to fall when the own-price elasticity is less than unity. Revenue from tobacco declines with the degree of complementarity, whereas it increases from tobacco because of complementarity; however, revenue from the consumption will increase, whereas it will increase in the case of alcohol as alcohol is substitutable. As the tax rate on marijuana will increase, the revenue through tax of all three products will increase, whereas the revenue collected from the consumption of alcohol falls because of the degree substitutability. Decriminalization of the possession of marijuana or other drugs eliminates the criminal status of the offence provision of the drug, whereas depenalization does not eliminate the criminal status of the possession of the drug. Criminal charges may prevent those who have been charged to obtain employment.

CHAPTER 5

The Prevention and Treatment of Alcohol Abuse

Abstract Various possibilities of prevention and treatment of alcohol abuse are discussed: government intervention in the abuse of alcohol, the effectiveness in the intervention of the abuse of alcohol, the treatment of alcohol abuse, the prevention and rehabilitation of alcohol abuse and harm minimization as a viable strategy. As the abuse of alcohol is widespread, the consequences may be severe to the physical and mental health of abusers of alcohol. As the social costs are high, it is important that there are adequate policies in place to reduce and minimize the harm of the abuse of alcohol. Hence, the effectiveness of various programmes of intervention and treatment is described. Harm minimization is described as a viable strategy to reduce the detrimental effect of alcohol abuse.

Keywords Government policies · Cumulative scientific evidence and government policies · Intervention and treatment · Prevention and rehabilitation · Harm minimization

1 Introduction

This chapter analyses various possibilities of prevention and treatment of alcohol abuse. This chapter is divided in five sections: (a) government intervention in the abuse of alcohol, (b) the effectiveness in the intervention of the abuse of alcohol, (c) the treatment of alcohol abuse,

J. Joshua, *The Economics of Addictive Behaviours Volume II*,
DOI 10.1007/978-3-319-54425-0_5

(d) the prevention and rehabilitation of alcohol abuse and (e) harm minimization as a viable strategy.

As the abuse of alcohol is widespread and the consequences may be severe to the physical and mental health of abusers of alcohol, and as the social costs are high, it is important that there are adequate policies in place to reduce and minimize the harm of the abuse of alcohol. Hence, the effectiveness of various programmes of intervention and treatment of alcohol abuse will be described, and finally harm minimization is described as a viable strategy to reduce the detrimental effect of alcohol abuse.

The behavioural disease of alcohol abuse results in numerous costs; it causes accidents and contributes to crime and violence, it causes productivity loss from episodic illness and eventual premature death. The abuse of alcohol also has repercussions on people other than the abuser of alcohol, such as family members through domestic violence or dysfunctional families, or in places of work through absenteeism and presenteeism, and through traffic accidents.

Such consequences of alcohol abuse create considerable costs so that policies of prevention and various types of treatment have been described. Various types of intervention and taxation policies to reduce the abuse of alcohol and its detrimental effects have also been described. However, as Kia-Keating et al. (2009) stated, alcohol-abusing youth have less motivation than adults to change the alcohol-abusing behaviour. Alcohol dependence has been defined in the Diagnostic and Statistical Manual of Mental Disorders (DSM-IV) as conditions which includes a persistent desire to drink alcohol, or unable to reduce the drinking of alcohol, experience withdrawal symptoms or to avoid withdrawing from the drinking of alcohol altogether. The effectiveness of various programmes of intervention of alcohol abuse and the treatment of alcohol abuse has been discussed, including prevention and rehabilitation programmes for alcohol abuse. As drug abuse, including the abuse of alcohol cannot be totally eliminated; harm minimization has been described as a viable strategy to reduce alcohol abuse.

Zachry et al. (2002) argued that treatments are effective in alleviating social and private costs; however, even though various treatments have been shown to be effective in reducing social and private costs, they appear to be underutilized, especially in the case of a combination of pharmacotherapy and psychotherapy in the treatment of alcohol abuse and dependency treatment.

Government Policies and Intervention in the Abuse of Alcohol

Measures to reduce alcohol consumption consist of four types of interventions: (1) adequate policies and supporting legislations, including excise duties, driving under the influence of alcohol, reduction or elimination of advertisements and restricted sales outlets; (2) legal enforcements of such laws, for example, frequent random breath testing which has to be supported with the appropriate penalties; (3) public awareness campaigns through the media and other outlets and (4) therapeutic intervention with high-risk alcohol abusers.

Policies to reduce the abuse of alcohol can operate at the level of production, supply, marketing and demand of alcohol. Policies to reduce the consumption of alcohol may include minimum legal purchasing age, limiting the hours and days of sales, restrictions on the level of outlet density, excise taxes on alcohol, lower the content of alcohol in drinks, a low blood alcohol content limit (BAC), random breath testing, treatment and detoxification.

Various policies can be used to reduce the consumption of alcohol, such as (1) policies to restrict the availability of alcohol, (2) policies to increase public awareness through advertising campaigns, (3) policies to spread knowledge and information about the use of alcohol, such as through education, (4) policies to reduce drink-driving, (5) policies to regulate the market of alcoholic beverages and (6) harm-minimization programmes and individual interventions.

Drug availability can be drastically reduced through various policy options; for example, vendor regulations, changing the legal classification of drug types and restrictions on advertising. In the case of legal drugs, such as tobacco and alcohol, availability is the accessibility or convenience, whereas in the case of illicit drugs, availability is largely determined by the search cost, that is, the time spent by buyers to complete illegal drug transactions. Policies to control supply are often too strict in regard to some illicit drugs and too permissive in regard to alcohol, considering the degree of harm that alcohol and illicit drugs are doing.

The relationship between the consumption of alcohol and restrictive policies may be bidirectional, that is, restrictive policies may restrict the level of alcohol, but the detrimental effect of heavy drinking of alcohol may also induce more restrictive policies. As restrictive policies reduce the consumption of alcohol, the detrimental effects of alcohol will also decline, including diseases such as liver cirrhosis. The drinking behaviour will also have different impact on the detrimental effects of drinking; for example, the drinking of wine with a dinner will have a lesser detrimental effect than binge drinking or heavy drinking.

Various control and intervention measures can be implemented: hours of sales, geographical density of sales outlets, alcohol interlocks, the labelling of drinks and publicity and education programmes. Whatever policies are adopted, they will have different effects on the consumption of drugs by different groups of consumers. Short-term binge drinkers will respond differently than long-term drinkers who drink at a hazardous level.

Sales of alcohol may be affected through pricing policies, the location of outlets, number and density of purchasing outlets, hours of opening, days of opening and randomized breath testing on the roadside. However, pricing policies in controlling the demand for alcohol are more successful than almost any other policies.

Public health policies to constrain the abuse of alcohol may use different measures. Awareness campaigns through education and training can be used; however, they have not been shown to be very effective. However, more effective policies are price increases through the imposition of an excise tax, restriction on the availability of alcoholic beverages such as trading hours, increasing the legal minimum drinking age.

The World Health Organization reports of 2002 and 2003 have linked substance use disorders to the abuse of alcohol, drugs and nicotine dependence and highlighted the various detrimental effects of alcohol abuse which have been described in Chapters 3 and 4 of this book. A stewardship-guided state contemplates to promote and protect the health of the general public and to reduce the inequalities of health within the nation. There are fewer restrictions on the consumption of alcohol in many low-income countries so that the alcohol industry is there free to expand their market at the cost of greater detrimental effects on the health of the general public. Countries still have a long way to go before they introduce adequate health policies to reduce the abuse and misuse of alcohol.

Governments worldwide proclaim that they intend to improve the well-being of the population, including people's health and a decline in the inequalities of health between social classes; however, healthcare does often not appear to be a top priority as many funds are provided for projects that do not improve the well-being of the public. Governments often attempt to negotiate a line between the well-being of the population of the nation and the profit of multinational corporations. An increase in the growth of GDP is often confused with an increase in the well-being of the nation. However, how an increase of the GDP will affect the well-being of the nation will depend on how the benefits of the increase in GDP have been distributed and whether the growth in GDP leads towards a sustainable economic growth.

Regarding the process of making decisions at the political level, "cost-effectiveness arguments only played a marginal role.... All kind of interests, often conflicting, had to be taken into account" (van Iwaarden, 1989, p. 1209) so that a "bureaucratic bargaining process does not always result in optimal solutions, and it is unlikely that cost-effectiveness arguments would play a predominant role" (van Iwaarden, 1989, p. 1209). Policies on alcohol should be seen within the context of public health policy to advocate and serve the health and well-being of the general public. A merger between science and practice would provide a more effective way to do the essential research as well as to introduce science into practice (Markowitz, 2000). In other words, to introduce science into political practice could create viable policies to increase the well-being of the nation.

Cumulative scientific evidence should be the basis for any governmental policy to control behavioural diseases, including the abuse of alcohol so that most of the ramifications of all the detrimental effects derived from human behaviours which cause behavioural diseases may be considered. Resource allocation should be based on scientific evidence which may ascertain the clinical effectiveness of given programmes. The effectiveness of policies has to be constantly evaluated; as the effectiveness of different policies will change over time, the optimum policy mix will also change with changes in the conditions.

To develop the right policies to reduce alcoholism, it is important to distinguish processes of initiation and processes of maintaining the drinking behaviour. As alcohol users drink over a longer period, they become addicted and so continue to drink to satisfy the physical need of their addiction. There are several views about the initiation of drinking alcohol. Some argue that the drinking of alcohol is a learned response to reduce distress. Dollard and Miller (1950) developed the concept of a delay of reward gradient which states that both rewards and punishments lose their effectiveness the further they are away in time; for example, a punishment that occurs sometimes in the future is less effective than an immediate punishment. As users of alcohol may experience a reduction in distress presently, they are less likely to worry about the adverse effects that the continued use of alcohol may cause as it lies into the distant future. Consumers generally discount future outcomes by comparing them with immediate consequences; such discounting is hyperbolic which implies that the rate of substitution in the short run is smaller than in the following periods; in other words, consequences in the present will be given greater importance than consequences which may lie in the future.

Policies have to take account of the misuse and the abuse of alcohol; both concepts may require differ policies. Misuse of alcohol may occur only once but has disastrous consequences, like getting drunk for the first time and then having a fatal car accident. Alcohol abuse however is evolving over a longer period which may eventually lead to addiction.

Furthermore, Cook and Reuter (2007) made the point that "alcohol cannot be balkanized from drugs" (p. 1185) because of cross-price elasticity between different drugs so that drug users may switch to a substitute drug if the drug of choice has an increase in price; for example, when the price of alcohol increases and if the cross-elasticity of marijuana for alcohol is large, then there may be a decline in the consumption of cannabis. In fact, there may be substitution as well as complementary effects. It may be argued that present policies in most countries are too lenient in regard to the use of tobacco products and alcohol abuse, and too harsh in regard to illicit drugs. If the United States has in excess of 500,000 inmates because of drug offences, as stated by Cook and Reuter (2007), then the drug control policies obviously are not very effective and there is an argument in favour of a more health-oriented policy.

The Effectiveness in the Intervention of the Abuse of Alcohol

A comprehension of the underlying processes of addiction and their treatment is vital before the high rate of mortality from the abuse of drugs can be reduced. A greater understanding implies that treatment for addiction can be more specifically directed towards specific cases. Efforts to prevent the abuse of alcohol may be best related to the level of harm that alcohol abuse may cause; thus, the greater the damage and harm caused, the more attention should be given. As the abuse of alcohol as a contributing factor of car accidents is substantial, that is, over one-third of mortality caused by car accidents involves the driving under the influence of alcohol, more attention should be paid to the problem of driving under the influence of alcohol.

The consequential social damage is not easily estimated; however, the detrimental effect on health and resulting diseases are more accurate (Rehm et al., 2003). Alcohol and illicit drugs cause costs which are multiple times greater than the taxes collected from legal drugs and revenues (Giesbrecht et al., 2006); however, as Giesbrecht et al. (2006) pointed out, effective interventions "are typically not widely supported and therefore difficult to implement and maintain" (p. 634). This is especially the case as alcohol is widely promoted and is part of the locally accepted culture.

Foxcroft (2006a) made the point that the effectiveness of interventions has to be assessed according to their epidemiological impact. An economic evaluation should consider the cost of intervention as well as the consequences of the implementation. Anderson and Baumberg (2006) found that there was a lack of evidence that interventions based in schools had a significant impact on the reduction of alcohol abuse. Likewise, Anderson et al. (2009) summarizing numerous systematic reviews concluded that classroom-based education is not very effective in reducing the detrimental effects of alcohol abuse. Despite of its lack of apparent effectiveness, school-based alcohol education is one of the most widely used approaches, especially in Europe, to reduce the abuse of alcohol.

The Treatment of Alcohol Abuse

Alcoholics who go through treatment first enter the stage of detoxification before real treatment can commence. However, if heavy drinking has been caused by depression, treatment which only focuses on the reduction of alcohol consumption is unlikely to be useful in the long term. Zachry et al. (2002) provided various situations under which pharmacological treatment has been successful in reducing alcohol abuse and dependence, especially when it has been used in conjunction with psychotherapy. Effective treatment will reduce the private as well as social costs of alcohol abuse; however, they argue that treatment of substance abuse is underutilized.

Pharmacogenetics can go a considerable way in reducing the detrimental effect of drug abuse. Pharmacogenetics is the combined study of pharmacokinetics and pharmacodynamics, the former is the study of individual differences in drug metabolism and the latter is the study of the drug response. Ethanol acts in a similar fashion as other drugs. Ethanol modulates the brain's reward system as it acts on the dopaminergic system and so will affect individual's behaviour. Sturgess et al. (2011) surveyed multiple pharmacogenetics studies which show "that response to pharmacotherapy for drug addiction is influenced by genetic factors" (p. 371).

Public health policies regarding the consumption of alcohol may be guided mainly by two separate criteria. First, the relationship between public revenue derived from alcohol and the public costs caused by alcohol-related problems. If consumers of alcohol are made liable for the detrimental effect of the consumption of alcohol, then this implies an increase in taxes on the consumption of alcohol. Second, policies have to be cost-effective to be viable.

The implementation of policies to decrease the burden of the abuse of alcohol, smoking and drug abuse may be at the personal level or the non-personal level. Personal interventions may be in the form of detoxification, nicotine replacement therapy or brief counselling. Non-personal intervention may be through the ban of advertising, the ban of smoking in public areas and other designated areas and the imposition of an excise tax. The most costly interventions are random breath testing because of the requirement for sobriety checkpoints and law enforcement officers, and brief interventions in primary care, whereas taxation was the most effective and cost-effective strategy where there was a high prevalence of heavy drinking, for example, in the Americas. On the other hand, tax policies were the least effective in regions where there is a low rate of heavy consumption of alcohol, for example, in South-East Asia (Chisholm et al., 2006).

The effectiveness of treatments of alcoholism has implications on clinical management and on health policy. Cost-effectiveness refers to the best clinical outcome at the least cost. Resources should be directed towards methods which are able to minimize harm which entails an assessment of the effectiveness of the use of the drugs as well as the costs of the methods used to reduce the use of drugs. Whereas any cigarette smoked is harmful to health, there are arguments in support that moderate alcohol consumption may be beneficial; for example, Rimm et al. (1991) argued that it lowers the risk of coronary heart disease in men. The harmful effect of alcohol comes from its abuse which may cause cirrhosis of the liver, or misuse, which may cause traffic accidents.

Various behavioural treatment methods have similar success in reducing the consumption of alcohol in the short term, regardless of whether they are cognitive behavioural therapies, motivational enhancement therapies, behavioural marital therapies or community reinforcements. Finney and Monahan (1996) confirmed the effectiveness of various treatment modalities which included stress management techniques, social-skill training and general counselling. However, their studies failed to find a relationship between effectiveness of treatments and their costs. Cost-effective treatment may reduce the social costs, including a reduction in the costs of medical care and lost wages (Hingson and Winter, 2003).

The Prevention and Rehabilitation of Alcohol Abuse

Decisions on the viability of the prevention of alcohol abuse require an understanding of the overall burden of alcohol abuse. Costs do impinge on the patient, the society and on the healthcare system, which includes the costs and benefits of various available therapies. A drug prevention programme has to be sustainable, and to be sustainable, it has to be scientifically and empirically based.

Preventative programmes have to be combined with evaluation to be able to assess the effectiveness of any preventative programmes so that programmes may be modified if necessary. Programmes that are shown to be ineffective should be phased out or modified as required. Inadequate ineffective programmes use up resources which could be allocated to more effective programmes. A sustainable programme has to be constantly monitored and evaluated; if necessary, appropriate changes have to be made during the duration of the programme.

Any prevention and rehabilitation programme has to be evaluated for its effectiveness so that resources can then be allocated towards the most effective programmes. Without appropriate evaluation and monitoring, resources are likely to be wasted. Prevention programmes should be guided by empirical and scientific evidence and not by industry groups who have a vested interest that the consumption of their products, may that be cigarettes, alcohol or soft drinks, not be reduced. After all, the harm that the consumption of such products causes is far greater than the benefits it creates in terms of employment, tax revenues, income or investment. As the profits of the liqueur, tobacco and soft drinks industries increase, there is a direct increase in the harm their products may cause; in other words, the social costs by far outweigh the private benefits that may occur.

Preventive interventions are thought to be generally highly cost-effective as they save considerable costs many years later. However, Ritter and Cameron (2006) found in their research on the efficiency and efficacy in the case of alcohol harm-reduction interventions that harm-reduction interventions to decrease traffic accidents were effective, but there were limited evidence in support of effectiveness and efficacy in the case of other alcohol harm-reduction interventions.

When the control of drugs is deemed to be impossible, governments often resort to prohibition as a viable alternative. However, the prohibition of drugs causes many problems that usually are thought to be associated with illicit drugs. Prohibition on drugs causes the supply curve for drugs to shift upwards. The enforcement, including possible fines and jail sentences, increases the cost of the supply of drugs. Prohibition also causes the demand curve of drugs to shift downwards as a result of possible penalties for the possession of drugs; however, "the downward shift is likely to be small relative to the upward shift" (Miron and Zwiebel, 1995, p. 176). Unless the elasticity of demand is greater than the elasticity of supply, prices under prohibition will necessarily increase. Miron and Zwiebel (1995) argued that "drug prohibition promotes violence" (p. 178). Most drug-related murders were "economic compulsive", or systemic, which refers to "battling over drug territory"; that is, crime committed to support their "drug habit" (p. 178).

Furthermore, "[n]o economic compulsive or systemic murders were reported relating to alcohol" (Miron and Zwiebel, 1995, p. 178). Prohibition to drugs makes it easier for a cartel to be established and thus reduces supply and increases price and real profits, instead of just quasi-rents to offset costs of law evasion. Effects of prohibition as Miron and Zwiebel (1995) pointed out are the increased accidental poisonings and an increase of property crime, because of the greater uncertainty about the quality of the drug and users of illicit drugs cannot complain about lack of quality of the drug as in the case of legal products. Property crimes are committed in support of supporting their drug addiction. The increase in price of the illicit drugs also increases the probability of increasing property crimes. The criminalization of the use of certain drugs also diverts police resources away from fighting other crimes.

Miron and Zwiebel (1991) pointed out that prohibition of alcohol may affect the consumption of alcohol in various ways. Prohibition increases the costs of supplies, including the costs of avoiding detection and punishment which causes a decline in consumption because of an increase in the equilibrium market price. Prohibition makes access to alcoholic beverages more difficult and so rises the search costs and also may lower the quality of alcohol. Miron and Zwiebel's (1991) main argument was that prohibition of alcohol was ineffective and argued further that this would also be the case with illegal drugs and mentioned various benefits of drug legalization (see further on the legalization of various drugs in volume III).

Of course, if remedies succeed to lower the rate of mortality from the abuse of licit drugs, such as from the use of alcohol or nicotine, or illicit drugs, or as a result of obesity, individuals will die eventually from different causes so that this would incur other health costs instead because of an increase in age-related diseases; but as age-related diseases occur later, there should be a net benefit accruing from a decline in alcohol-related diseases.

Harm Minimization as a Viable Strategy

The abuse of drugs, including alcohol, cannot be eliminated, although it can be reduced. If this is the case, then policies of harm minimization might follow. If policies to reduce demand and supply are not successful, harm-minimization programmes could be adopted to substitute for policies which have failed or such programmes could be used in addition and they could be used for legal as well as for illicit drugs.

Nicotine, alcohol and illicit drugs are all psychoactive substances which affect the user's mind and body; but their cultural acceptance and their legal status differ. Their legal status is based on cultural perception grounded in history and ideology, rather than on scientific evidence. Policies regarding psychoactive substances may be better aimed towards harm minimization so that any policies should be subject to evaluation to determine which policies are most efficient.

Policies to reduce psychoactive substance abuse should aim for harm minimization and based on scientific evidence. Public health policies should be more preventive rather than merely reactive in their policy orientation. Harm-minimization policies may be tailored specifically to different groups of alcohol consumers as they will be affected by such policies in different ways. However, to adopt different policies for different groups is a difficult task.

Harms caused through the abuse of alcohol which are addressed by a harm-minimization programme consist of three types: traffic accidents caused by drink-driving, injury and violence and social harms (see Ritter and Cameron, 2006). Harm-reduction programmes in the case of illicit drugs are mainly concerned with the harms caused by the sharing of needles which may result in the transmission of HIV and other infectious diseases. Needle syringe programmes have been shown to be cost-effective (World Health Organisation, 2004c; Wodak and Cooney, 2005). A harm-reduction strategy may involve the addition of thiamine to liquor which may prevent the development of Korsakoff's psychosis.

Harm-minimization programmes only gained significance during the early 1980s and were mainly concerned with the abuse of illicit drugs and were first used in Australia, Canada, the Netherlands, Switzerland and the United Kingdom. Policies of harm minimization or harm reduction are concerned with programmes that intend to reduce the harm of drugs, rather than the use of drugs, although to minimize the harm may eventually lead to a decline in the use of drugs as well. The point here is that much of the population are living within a drug culture, whether by the use of alcohol, nicotine or illicit drugs so that as it is difficult to eliminate their consequences, harm may at least be minimized. In this case, programmes such as methadone maintenance which reduce harm through the decrease of the use of alcohol are not strictly speaking harm-reduction programmes. O'Brien et al. (2012) advocated that the aim of reducing the harm caused by alcohol should be supported by policies of introducing alcohol-screening programmes in emergency department, something that is relatively rarely done.

McBride et al. (2004) evaluated the School Alcohol Harm Reduction Programme and found that young people were able to process harm-reduction messages adequately. Harm-reduction programmes which were not emphasizing solely the non-use or delayed use generally resulted in greater reductions in the consumption of alcohol than programmes which promoted abstinence and delayed use. A further finding of this study was that intervention students were far less likely to consume alcohol at a hazardous level during follow-up occasions.

Drug strategies to be effective should be an integral policy of four strategies to aim for harm reduction: first, the reduction of the spread of communicable diseases, such as HIV/AIDS, and the prevention of death through overdose. Second, to prevent or to reduce the prevalence of drug use, that is, to provide the relevant information so that potential drug users may be able to make health choices and to provide drug users the chance to reduce or eliminate their use of drugs. Third, rehabilitation of drug users and to reduce the use of drugs; such treatment may include medical care, methadone programmes and outpatient programmes for those who have taken drugs. Fourth, the enforcement of the relevant laws which are dealing with the use and abuse of drugs, including the targeting of drug dealing and other criminal elements. The four policies on drug abuse will have to be community based.

CHAPTER 6

Legal Remedies to Reduce Alcohol Consumption

Abstract Legal remedies to reduce the consumption of alcohol will be discussed, including conditions of sales, price promotion, randomized breath testing, means to prevent driving under the influence and the banning of advertising of alcoholic beverages. Various strategies to reduce the consumption of alcohol will be addressed. First, policies directed at behavioural modification may be directed at individual abusers of alcohol, such as remedies against drink-driving or brief interventions during primary care to reduce alcohol abuse. Second, corrective policies may be directed at problems caused by the misuse of alcohol, such as fatal car accidents. Third, preventive policies may be directed towards the public at large, such as regulations on advertising of alcoholic beverages, restrictions on sales and the implementation of an effective taxation policy.

Keywords Educational impact · Conditions of sales · Price promotion · Randomized breath testing · Ban of advertising

1 Introduction

This chapter will discuss the legal remedies to reduce the consumption of alcohol. The chapter is divided in five sections: (a) educational impact on the reduction of alcohol abuse; (b) conditions of sales: purchasing outlets, number of locations and density, and hours of opening; (c) price promotion and discounts; (d) randomized breath testing and other means to

J. Joshua, *The Economics of Addictive Behaviours Volume II*,
DOI 10.1007/978-3-319-54425-0_6

prevent driving under the influence and (e) ban of advertising of alcoholic beverages.

Policies on harm minimization of course will differ depending on whether the psychoactive drugs are legal or illicit. There are greater possibilities when dealing with legal drugs, such as nicotine and alcohol. Thus, cigarette packaging and alcoholic beverage containers may be labelled with warnings and distribution may be restricted. Containers of alcoholic products could carry warning labels describing the harmful effects of the abuse of alcohol (Anderson and Baumberg, 2006, p. 16), or packaging may include advice of how much may be consumed at a save level.

There are various strategies to prevent or to reduce the consumption of alcohol. There are essentially three different ways in which policies can reduce the detrimental effects of alcohol abuse. First, policies directed at behavioural modification may be directed at individual abusers of alcohol, such as remedies against drink-driving or brief interventions during primary care to reduce alcohol abuse. Second, corrective policies may be used directed at problems caused by the misuse of alcohol, such as fatal car accidents. Third, preventive policies may be directed towards the public at large, such as regulations on advertising of alcoholic beverages, restrictions of sales through density of outlets, trading hours, minimum drinking age, maximum legal blood alcohol concentration, age limit for the purchase of alcoholic beverages and the implementation of an effective taxation policy. Such policies can be used together to further reduce the abuse of alcohol. This chapter gives an outline of the various available policy instruments.

Educational Impact on the Reduction of Alcohol Abuse

Educational programmes should be introduced as a policy to increase awareness of the problems involved in abusing alcohol which could support other policies; education programmes alone however would not be very successful. Even though prevention programmes implemented within a school setting can reach a large audience at a relatively low cost, their effectiveness has been disputed. According to Giesbrecht (2007), present education programmes to reduce alcohol are not very effective. Giesbrecht (2007) made the point that there is a lack "of evidence of the effectiveness of education and persuasion in reducing consumption, curtailing high-risk drinking or reducing damage from alcohol" (p. 1345). Foxcroft (2006b) also found insufficient evidence that shows education, awareness and persuasion methods to be effective to prevent the abuse of alcohol amongst young people. However, the detrimental effects of excessive alcohol consumption are well known and vary policies to reduce the harm are known to be effective.

On the other hand, Teesson et al. (2012) found that in Australia, school-based prevention programmes, mostly based on social learning principles, have been effective in reducing alcohol, tobacco and cannabis at follow-up, in contrast to most other school-based prevention programmes which were mostly ineffective. However, Caulkins et al. (2004) found that the social benefits resulting from school-based drug-prevention programmes were greater than the costs of the programmes, while the benefits in the case of licit drugs were greater than in the case of illicit substances, perhaps by twice as much.

Even though educational interventions have been largely ineffective in reducing alcohol abuse, such educational interventions may increase awareness of the detrimental effects of the abuse of alcohol, and so may make restrictions and legislations more acceptable to the public. Behavioural diseases have been caused not only by people's behaviour but much of such behaviour is habitual so that it has been difficult to provide effective behavioural change to effect a reduction in the abuse of alcohol, the smoking of cigarettes and the use of illicit drug. The approaching tsunami of fatness that is approaching society as a result of overeating is another example of many. Lifestyle is not only associated with behavioural diseases but modern lifestyle is for many people sedentary so that many do not adhere to a healthy lifestyle. Hence, Olshansky et al. (2005) argued that today's children may live a shorter life than their parents.

Overall, school-based intervention programmes generally have only a small effect or none at all, on the abuse of alcohol. School-based programmes may be more successful in reducing alcohol abuse when such programmes are combined with other policies and strategies so that such school programmes could be used in support of other policies. The promotion of health education through the school curriculum to spread knowledge about behavioural diseases could also assist in reducing such diseases provided teachers are adequately qualified in this area. An education programme would mainly involve making people aware of the risks involved in the abuse of alcohol. A more difficult task is to change the attitude towards the consumption of alcohol so that the consumption of alcohol may decline to prevent the abuse of alcohol.

Public information campaigns generally have been ineffective in reducing the abuse of alcohol. Advising potential consumers of alcohol of the risk involved in association with alcohol is not very effective in reducing high-risk alcohol consumption and so do not reduce tax revenue collected by the government as it does not reduce sales of alcohol. However, as Giesbrecht (2007) argued, such interventions increase "the profile of alcohol and potentially set the stage for further initiatives" (p. 1346). However, media campaign to reduce drink-driving has been more effective, especially when conducted in conjunction with other drink-driving strategies, such as breath testing, lowering the blood alcohol concentration (BAC) or suspension of the driving licence (Elder et al., 2004).

The alcohol industry rejects government intervention in the marketing strategies of alcohol companies and specifically rejects the imposition of health warning labels and argued that to frighten consumers will not be effective (Zachry et al., 2002). The alcohol industry formed the Beverage Information Council as a response to the US Department of the Treasury study which concluded that more education of the public regarding the effect of the consumption of alcohol was required; especially, awareness of the detrimental effect on pregnancy should be increased. It was argued that education was more effective than "simplistic regulatory approaches" (Gavaghan, 1983, p. 11). However, as discussed in the "Educational impact on the reduction of alcohol abuse" section, the educational impact on the reduction of alcohol abuse has not been highly significant.

Conditions of Sales and Purchasing Outlets: Number of Locations and Density, and Hours of Opening

The availability of alcohol may be reduced by regulating the outlets of sales, the number of locations, density, opening hours, as well as the sales prices; however, various methods to reduce the abuse of alcohol are opposed by the alcohol industry. A greater density of alcohol outlets increases the consumption of alcohol and with it increases the detrimental effects of the abuse of alcohol. The extension of trading hours also increases the consumption of alcohol, whereas a decline in the trading hours will reduce sales and reduce the detrimental effects of the abuse of alcohol, such as violence and homicide (Duailibi et al., 2007); for example, after the Municipal Act of 2001 prohibited the opening of bars from 10 p.m. to 6 a.m., the rate of homicide declined considerable in Diadema situated within the São Paulo metropolitan area. To reduce the density of alcohol outlets and reduced hours of trading are expected to reduce injury, public disorder and violence. Carpenter (2005) found that a decline in the availability of alcohol and a higher minimum level of drinking age were associated with a decline of arrest for disorderly conduct and vandalism amongst 18–20-year olds.

The types of outlets of alcohol also have different impacts on the consumption of alcohol, hence the purchase of alcoholic beverages in supermarkets as compared with consumption of alcohol in bars. The number of alcohol outlets in a specific area is often decided on the assumption of market forces, rather than on the basis of the protection of public health. The level of alcohol consumption also relates to the sales price. Wagenaar et al. (2009) found that a 1% increase in the prices of beer, wine and spirits leads to a decline in consumption of beer by approximately 0.46%, of wine by 0.69% and of spirits by 0.80%, and consequentially the prevalence of violence has also decreased.

Popova et al. (2012) found that a privatization of the alcohol-retailing system in Canada would increase the cost of alcohol between 6% and 12% and the consumption of alcohol would increase from 10% to 20%. They found that for health and economic reasons, governments should continue to be the dominant force in the retailing of alcohol.

Legal drugs may be taxed, their sales may require a licence and there may be other regulations. The imposition of tax on alcohol may reduce externalities. In the case of illicit drugs, this is not an option. The costs of law enforcement to combat the traffic of illicit drugs take the majority of the budget allocated to the control of drugs. The major reason is that to make the production, distribution and sales of certain drugs illegal makes them a "lucrative" business; even though the risk increases for those engaged in the illicit drug trade, the profits also increase.

A more restrictive alcohol policy will reduce the consumption of alcohol and also has an effect on drinking habit, that is, the frequency, place and the time distribution of drinks. However, in many situations, regulations are not strictly enforced.

Price Promotions and Discounts

Other policy options which may be used to reduce the abuse of alcohol are bans on price promotions and bans on discounts. Different policy options will affect different groups of drinkers differently, so Meier et al. (2009) pointed out that "minimum pricing policies tend to affect harmful drinkers proportionately more, but young hazardous drinkers less than drinkers in general" (p. 391); hence, pricing policies will have a different impact on the detrimental effect of alcohol consumption, such as the rate of crime, detrimental effects on health and loss of productivity at work.

Anderson et al. (2009) found that policies controlling the marketing through price and availability were more effective than other policies in reducing the harm caused by alcohol misuse.

Randomized Breath Testing and Other Means to Prevent Driving under the Influence

The consumption of alcohol contributes greatly to road traffic accidents, injury and death because the consumption of alcohol impairs cognitive skills, vision and reaction time. Under the influence of alcohol, people are more likely to engage in risky behaviour such as speeding and other careless behaviour. However, various policies can be introduced to prevent driving under the influence of alcohol.

The BAC is the proportion of alcohol within a given volume of blood measured in grams per 100 ml of blood. The prevailing permissible BAC which represents the concentration of alcohol (ethanol) in the blood usually is set in most countries at 0.5 g/l or 0.05% while in charge of a vehicle; even though in Canada the permissible BAC is 0.05%, the criminal code penalty has been set at 0.08%, whereas the maximum BAC level for drivers in Europe is 0.5 g/l (except for the United Kingdom, Ireland and Luxembourg). However, the BAC could be lowered to 0.2 g/l as driving skills begin to impair as soon as the BAC is above zero (Anderson and Baumberg 2006, p. 145; citing Moskowitz and Fiorentino, 2000). The lowering of the permissible BAC level for young drivers and for repeat offenders, possible to zero, has been shown to be effective.

Various policies may be introduced to reduce drink-driving, such as random breath testing, mandated treatment for drink-driving and alcohol locks to prevent drink-driving. When random breath testing is in place, police stop drivers at random in order to check on the driver's blood alcohol content; all drivers may also be stopped at sobriety checkpoints for a BAC check. Such checks have been shown to be effective in reducing road fatalities and injuries resulting from traffic accidents which are related to the consumption of alcohol. However, regulations and enforcements have to be applied on a frequent and consistent basis so that drivers will realize that there is a real possibility of apprehension. Funds can also be set aside for treatment and rehabilitation.

Mandated treatment for drink-driving may be another option to reduce the social costs of driving under the influence of alcohol. Alcohol-related interventions and treatment will increase their effectiveness if they are combined with non-specific interventions; for example, the revoking or suspending of driver's licenses. A graduated driver licence programme will also help. The use of alcohol ignition interlocks which prevents a person with a BAC above the legal limit to start the car engine in the case of repeat offenders of drink-driving has also been able to reduce drink-driving. It places an interlock in the ignition so that drivers have to pass a breathalyser test before the car can be started, preferably together with random retest while the car engine is running.

The effectiveness of random breath testing depends largely on driver's perception of the probability of being apprehended. Thus, random breath testing has to be frequent so that the chance of being apprehended is relatively high. Random breath testing may serve as deterrence to drivers not to abuse alcohol and drive concurrently and so may reduce the detrimental effects of alcohol abuse. A nation-wide campaign was conducted in Australia to reduce drink-driving and between 1981 and 1992 reduced alcohol-related road fatalities "from 44% to 29% of all road crash deaths" (Commonwealth Department of Health and Aged Care, 2001, p. 11).

Willenbring (2014) made the point that screening and brief counselling for drinkers who are at-risk during ambulatory primary care are relatively cost-effective and also show a considerable degree of efficacy and advocated the implementation of them outside of the medical context; however, the efficacy of screening and brief intervention in emergency departments or hospitals have not been shown to be effective. One of the reasons which Willenbring (2014) pointed out is that, for example, changes in drink-driving occur weeks before the beginning of the treatment. Orford et al. (2006) and Penberthy et al. (2007) made similar points.

Problems have to be solved at the source or cause, that is, before something will eventuate, rather than after something has occurred. To confine drunk drivers in jail may be a deterrent for some in the future, but it does not help those who have died as a result of drink-driving. Reckless and irresponsible driving must be dealt with appropriately but some governments are reluctant to solve the problem of drink-driving adequately with sufficient enforcement, including with the appropriate driving education. Kenkel (1996) argued that the optimal alcohol tax rate would be much lower if the apprehension of drivers under the influence of alcohol would be much more certain and the penalties severe enough to deter driving under the influence of alcohol. Thus, the effectiveness of legal remedies to reduce the consumption of alcohol depends on the optimal combination of available policies.

Ban of Advertising of Alcoholic Beverages

One of the most harmful drugs, alcohol, is also the most advertised one. Adolescents are brought up within an intoxicating culture, where people are surrounded by drug abuses on a daily basis. As advertisements of such drugs increase, their consumption increases together with the resulting mortality and diseases. The increase in the consumption of alcohol then increases the profits of the corporations who produce and distribute such drugs. Therefore, there may be a case for restricting the use of advertisements for any drugs, such as alcohol; in much the same way as in many countries, the advertising for cigarettes has also been banned.

The effects of exposure to constant advertising are cumulative so that the consumption of alcohol will increase, especially amongst adolescents who acquire an attitude that drinking is fun. Exposure to marketing of alcohol will lower the age when adolescents become first initiated into the use of alcohol and also will increase the quantity of alcohol consumed. The earlier adolescents will start to drink alcohol, the more they are likely to drink in later years. Marketing plays an important role in finding replacement drinkers and for expanding the drinking population in emerging economies.

Other marketing strategies pursued by the alcohol industry will also increase the demand for alcohol, such as the developments of new brands and products. Anderson et al. (2009) gave a brief summary of various policies on the consumption of alcohol. To ban the promotion of alcoholic beverages would reduce the consumption of alcohol; however, self-regulation by the alcohol industry has not been successful in Australia (Jones et al., 2008).

The market of alcohol is subjected to competing messages, those that want to promote the sales of alcoholic beverages and those that want to constrain them. Anderson et al. (2009) made the point that industry-funded educational programmes encourage positive views about alcohol and the alcohol industry. Similarly, Smith et al. (2006) came to the same conclusion. Advertisements about alcoholic beverages portray the consumption of alcohol as part of a normal lifestyle. The sponsorship by the alcohol industry of events of sport venue has the same aim, that is, to promote their product and thereby is further seen as part of normal people's normal lifestyle.

Chisholm et al. (2004) found that population-wide strategies are more cost-effective where there are higher rates of alcohol abuse whereas strategies which are specifically targeted are more effective where there are lower rates of alcohol abuse. Chisholm et al. (2004) argued that priority should be given to the banning of advertising of alcohol and taxation policy, because of the high probability of cost savings. They also found that increasing the minimum legal age of drinking to 21 years of age, brief interventions, control of licensing, random breath testing together with drink-driving campaigns were also cost-effective. However, residential treatment for the dependence of alcohol has not been shown to be effective. They suggested that the detrimental effect of alcohol abuse could be decreased "by a third with the selection of interventions that have been evaluated" (p. 1654) in their study.

Overall, policies to prevent drink-driving were successful; however, this was not the case of school-based education. An increase in the price of alcohol, restricting the availability and banning the advertising of alcohol were the most cost-effective policies (Anderson et al., 2009). However, many interventions concentrate on drug use regardless of the prevailing evidence of harm caused. Advertising, prices, promotion and sponsorship by drug companies or the minimum legal purchasing age are national or provincially enacted, although the enforcement is generally a matter for local authorities. On the other hand, hours and days of trading, number of licences and the density of outlets are generally controlled at the local level. Hence, to make various regulations more effective, better coordination between national and local authorities may be required.

CHAPTER 7

The Market and the Social and Private Costs of Alcohol Abuse

Abstract This chapter discusses the market and its effect on public health. The harmonization of international trade makes alcoholic beverages cheaper; for example, the European Commission's internal and competition policies try to establish a common market for alcoholic beverages so that some European countries are hampered in establishing a more health-oriented policy in regard to the consumption of alcohol. The abuse of alcohol creates various external costs, including public health costs. Estimates of private and social costs can be used to target specific problems of alcohol abuse. One way to assess the social costs of alcohol abuse is to make a comparative analysis of the costs of healthcare of abusers of alcohol and of non-abusers of alcohol.

Keywords International trade · Social and private cost of alcohol abuse · Effect of alcohol abuse · Unemployment · Workplace

1 Introduction

This chapter deals with the market and the social and private costs of alcohol abuse. The chapter is divided in two sections: (a) international trade and public health and (b) the social and private costs of alcohol abuse.

The harmonization of international trade makes alcoholic beverages cheaper and therefore may have detrimental effects on public health; for

J. Joshua, *The Economics of Addictive Behaviours Volume II*,
DOI 10.1007/978-3-319-54425-0_7

example, the European Commission's internal and competition policies try to establish a common market for alcoholic beverages so that some European countries are hampered in establishing a more health-oriented policy in regard to the consumption of alcohol.

A description of the social and private costs of alcohol abuse will then follow. The abuse of alcohol creates various external costs, including public health costs, loss in productivity, and an increase in unemployment, crime, car accidents and premature death. The human capital and the friction approach have been explained to assess loss in productivity due to alcohol abuse. Estimates of private and social costs can be used to target specific problems of alcohol abuse. Alcohol abuse may also increase cost of obstetric and gynaecological patients due to foetal alcohol syndrome, increases in abortion or increased admissions in maternity hospitals. One way to assess the social costs of alcohol abuse is to make a comparative analysis of the costs of healthcare of abusers of alcohol and of non-abusers of alcohol. The next chapter will discuss the economic remedies to reduce alcohol abuse.

Markets, International Trade and Public Health

Most mainstream economists argue that when all the relevant information is available, then consumer sovereignty shall prevail. However, even though much information is available, important information needed for an informed decision may be difficult to obtain. Furthermore, the market is distorted, including through the advertising by the leading corporations, of the tobacco, food and alcohol industries.

Kenkel (1996) argued that the greater availability of information about the consequence of excessive alcohol consumption would eliminate to some extent the rationale for alcohol taxes. However, such drugs as alcohol are not normal goods, but rather many users are subject to addiction which is satisfied within a given social context. Furthermore, available information is often ignored as the consequences of the abuse of alcohol are not certain and lie too far into the future. His main argument is that the availability of more information would reduce the optimum tax rate. However, heavy and alcohol-dependent drinkers will react differently to available information and have lower price elasticity than occasional drinkers, even if such occasional drinkers consume on some occasions heavily. Dependents lack the ability to make a rational choice, and if they do, they often do not have the will power to follow-up on their choices (see Becker et al. 1991). Once consumers of drugs have become addicted, their behaviour cannot be assumed to be rational so that the rational choice model as assumed by mainstream economists loses its applicability.

The objective of the European Commission has been to create a common market for alcoholic beverages whereby the production is performed by those with the greatest comparative advantage. However, health policies are often ignored in common market policies. Government officials are inclined to take decisions which invoke the least political resistance so that those with the weakest or no lobbyists to represent them will usually miss out. Maynard and O'Brien (1982) explained that "Unfortunately the adoption of this policy brings with it an unfortunate predicted consequence: the overall effect of the price changes will be that consumption will rise. Thus, harmonization [of the European Commission policy] may increase the social costs arising from alcohol abuse" (p. 242), and they made the further point that the dominance of the finance ministries in questions on taxes on alcohol will have detrimental effects on public health. Hence, questions that have multidisciplinary effects should be guided by decision-makers who have themselves a multidisciplinary background or who draw decision makers from multiple disciplinary backgrounds so that all important relevant interests may be considered (Laranjeira and Mitsuhiro, 2010).

The European Commission's internal market and competition policies have the effect to remove barriers to trade between member countries. Another policy is the tax harmonization between member countries; both policies will tend to decrease the prices of alcoholic beverages and consequently, there may be an increase in the demand of alcoholic beverages and therefore an increase in alcohol abuse so that there will be an increase in social as well as economic costs.

As there are external costs involved in the consumption of drugs, such as alcohol, it cannot be argued that the free market will automatically achieve the best possible outcome. Various studies have tried to assess such external costs (Heien and Pittman, 1993; Cnossen, 2007; Richardson and Crowley, 1994).

Similarly, the unregulated market of alcohol in Brazil has contributed to the deterioration of public health in Brazil (Laranjeira and Mitsuhiro, 2010). The Brazilian market of alcoholic beverages is highly unregulated with a high concentration of alcohol outlets; perhaps not surprisingly, 25% of the Brazilian population resort to binge drinking (Laranjeira and Mitsuhiro, 2010). However, the advertising of alcoholic beverages is restrained, and since June 2008, the permissible level of the BAC is zero with severe penalties if driving under the influence of alcohol. Furthermore, the purchase of alcohol is prohibited by persons of less than 18 years of age; however, this is often not enforced (Laranjeira and Mitushiro, 2010).

To prevent behavioural diseases, such as alcohol abuse, from occurring or at least to try to reduce them implies that advertisements of such harmful substances may be restricted or altogether eliminated. However, effective alcohol control policies are often in conflict with international trade agreements which consider alcoholic beverages as normal commodities and so try to make them easier available. Prices of alcoholic beverages may be increased through a minimum price policy and increase in taxation, or the banning of advertising; however, such policies are often hampered by international trade agreements or competition regulations.

As international trade policies regard alcoholic beverages as ordinary goods, it makes it more difficult to implement policies to control the consumption of alcohol. International trade agreements may hamper effective control of alcohol abuse; for example, the economic integration of the European Union makes it more difficult for individual countries to introduce restrictive policies as they may conflict with European policies which promote free trade between member countries.

Political decision-making processes are subject to powerful vested interests so that interests of public health are not the only concern as policies on alcohol control are subject to competing interests and ideologies. The implementation of effective health policies at the national and international levels may often be prevented because of vested interests and international trade agreements. The harmful diseases resulting from alcohol abuse can only be reduced with effective policies implemented by countries in coordination. Policies to reduce behavioural diseases, including the abuse of alcohol, are generally not based on scientific evidence and many policies have not been evaluated for their effectiveness.

However, taxes on alcoholic beverages are relatively effective in reducing the detrimental effect of alcohol abuse. World Health Organization (2004a) found this to be the case in Western Europe in reducing ill health or premature death due to alcohol misuse. A comprehensive international health policy on alcohol may be introduced because alcohol travels across borders; otherwise, some international trade agreements may prevent the promotion of health and the prevention of the lowering of diseases from the abuse of alcohol. International trade agreements may not be implemented when they contravene best-practised public health policies.

The Social and Private Costs of Alcohol Abuse

The excessive consumption of alcohol creates various external costs, including the public health costs; such costs may be covered at least to some extent by the imposition of excise taxes; even though such an excise tax would affect all alcohol consumers indiscriminately regardless whether the consumers drink in excess or not. According to economic welfare theory, consumers of alcohol obtain positive net benefits; that is, there is consumer surplus. Consumers of alcohol may over-consume and when the abuse of alcohol becomes a behavioural disease, then consumer surplus is negative and alcohol consumption as a behavioural disease is not welfare enhancing which can only be increased by overcoming alcohol abuse as a disease. In this case, abusers of alcohol will gain when an excise tax is imposed on the consumption of alcohol. They gain firstly because their expenditures on alcohol decline; secondly, they gain because they will experience a decline in the internal costs of alcohol abuse.

An increase in the rate of an excise tax on the prices of alcoholic beverages may decrease the demand of alcohol, but as Cook et al. (2005) pointed out, this "may be the result of both a reduction in the prevalence of alcohol abuse and the prevalence of moderate drinking, with opposite effects on mortality rates" (p. 278). Abuse of alcohol may cause liver cirrhosis, accidents and violence, but there may also be health benefits for middle-age people as it is associated with a decline in heart disease and stroke (Corrao et al., 2000). Cook et al. (2005) found that a 1% reduction in per capita consumption of alcohol has "little net effect on mortality in middle age" (p. 278), and as there are no health benefits in drinking alcohol "for younger people, and considerable risks", they "conclude that the public-health case for increased alcohol taxation is strong" (p. 278). Hence, an excise tax on the consumption of alcohol appears to be a sensible policy; however, governments often pursue priorities which are not necessarily promoting the well-being of the public at large. Nevertheless, as Wagenaar et al. (2009) pointed out, excise and sales taxes are the most widely used policies to affect the sales prices in reducing the consumption of alcohol.

The detrimental effects of alcohol abuse and the associated costs may be assessed through multidimensional effects on health. An analysis of the cost of illness may include healthcare loss in productivity, costs associated with crime and motor vehicle accidents and premature death. The driving under the influence of alcohol may cause external costs through various ways; there may be injuries to the drunken drivers and to others, there may be loss of indirect utility from suffering lost time for work and leisure. Car accidents will cause property damage; there may be the cost of medical and emergency treatment. There is a loss in productivity and consequently a reduction in wages and therefore less tax revenue collected by the government.

The social costs of the abuse of alcohol are those that are imposed by the alcohol abusers on third parties. Not all problems caused by the abuse of alcohol relate to alcohol dependence which only comprises a small fraction of the problems caused by alcohol abuse. There are numerous mental, physical and social problems which are caused by the abuse of alcohol.

Loss in productivity is a major social cost of alcohol abuse resulting from reduced efficiency, absence due to sickness, presenteeism, absenteeism, unemployment, or premature death or disability. There are costs of alcohol abuse resulting from traffic, material damage from accidents, hospitalization, research and public campaigns. There are costs of alcohol abuse to private insurance for damages caused by the abuse of alcohol, such as traffic accidents and healthcare. There are also costs of alcohol abuse, such as social insurance payments for unemployment, disability, sickness, etc. caused by the abuse of alcohol. The insurance industry does not operate completely on free market principles; for example, there are barriers to entry and numerous regulations. Insurance companies generally cannot discriminate against alcoholics but may do so against smokers in many countries.

It may be assumed that the level of external costs will increase with the level of the abuse of alcohol. However, costs caused by the inappropriate use of alcohol may not meet the clinical definition of alcohol abuse; costs may occur because of a single episode of intoxication, whereas the clinical definition of alcohol abuse involves the regular heavy consumption of alcohol.

The detrimental effects deriving from the abuse of alcohol are well known; however, the actual costs are less certain. Nevertheless, here are some estimates. "The total tangible cost of alcohol to EU society in 2003 was estimated to be €125 bn (€79 bn–€220 bn), equivalent to 1.3% GDP" (Anderson and Baumberg, 2006, p. 47). The intangible costs, that is, pain, suffering and loss of life resulting from the abuse of alcohol, were in 2003 "estimated to be €270 bn, with other ways of valuing the same harms producing estimates between €150 bn and €760 bn" (Anderson and Baumberg, 2006, p. 47). Such estimates are subject to a wide margin of error; nevertheless, they are more likely to be underestimates (Anderson and Baumberg, 2006, p. 47). In Australia, the estimated economic costs of the misuse and abuse of alcohol was A$4.7 billion in 1992 which was 24% of the total economic costs of drug abuse of A$18.8 billion due to premature deaths, loss of productivity at work, law enforcement and costs of treatment (Collins and Lapsley, 1996). Alcohol abuse is a major public health problem in the United States (Carpenter and Dobkin, 2009, 2011) so that the social costs of alcohol abuse are substantial; for example, 41% of death in traffic accidents was caused by drink-driving in 2002 in the United States.

Further costs that may be included in an evaluation of the social costs of alcohol abuse may include the costs of the police administration and the judicial system, the costs of public health campaigns, including the administrative costs and cost of research. Such cost-of-illness studies can be utilized as a precursor to drug policy evaluation, especially cost–benefit analysis.

van Gils et al. (2010) found that economic evaluations underreport the true social cost of alcohol abuse. From a healthcare perspective, only costs pertaining to healthcare are relevant; on the other hand, a social perspective includes losses due to a decline in productivity, an increase in crime, costs of law enforcement and rehabilitation if provided, as well as healthcare costs.

Most studies use the human capital approach to assess cost estimates of drug policies, mainly using forgone productivity and forgone income. Studies by Collins et al. (2006) used a demographic approach by comparing an alternative population in which no substance-related death occurred. The interpretation of the costs of substance abuse with cost estimates may also depend on new epidemiological findings so that knowledge about the detrimental effects of drug and alcohol abuse is constantly raised; hence, many detrimental effects remain underreported for a considerable time; for example, foetal alcohol syndrome has in more recent years been increasing because its cause is now more traced back to the abuse of alcohol whereas previously it was underreported or attributed to other causes. Although there are considerable uncertainties about studies in cost estimation, such studies can identify various information gaps and may indicate new approaches for future research (see Single, 2009). Cost estimates can assist in targeting specific problems of drug and alcohol abuse and can improve on policies and provide better quality control.

Over half of the economic costs resulting from alcohol abuse are associated with lost productivity (Booth and Feng, 2002). Mullahy and Sindelar (1991) found that greater unemployment and lower wages was associated with a lifetime diagnosis of an alcohol disorder. However, French and Zarkin (1995) and Zarkin et al. (1998) found that a moderate use of alcohol was associated with higher salary than either heavy users of alcohol or abstainers. Booth and Feng (2002) in a longitudinal study of at-risk drinkers of alcohol in the six southern states in the United States found that the chance of at-risk drinkers who drank seven or more drinks per day was six times greater to be unemployment than those who drank less than seven drinks per day.

Of course, there is also a reciprocal relationship between the abuse of alcohol and unemployment; on the one hand, alcohol abuse may lead to unemployment but unemployment may also lead to the abuse of alcohol, perhaps partly because of depression, and partly because people tend to fill in the time available with mundane activities, such as drinking alcohol, which may then increase over the time of unemployment. Mullahy and Sindelar (1994a, b) found that alcoholism reduces participation in the work force amongst males of prime working age and consequently reduces their income. In this case, the consumption of alcohol and unemployment may reinforce each other; the longer the period of unemployment, the greater the consumption of alcohol which then may lead to more unemployment. Booth and Feng (2002) argued that a high level of consumption of alcohol is as important as education as a predictor of employment in other studies.

Rayner and Chetwynd (1987) made the point that costs of obstetric and gynaecological patients are also to some extent related to the consumption of alcohol; for example, it may induce foetal alcohol syndrome. Excess alcohol consumption may also be involved in unwanted pregnancies which will then either increase the rate of abortions or admissions to maternity hospitals. The excess use of alcohol may also lead towards premature ageing and hence to an increase in geriatric treatment. Abusers of alcohol generally only seek medical treatment when their symptoms from alcohol abuse are severe; hence, hospital treatment would increase but medical treatment from a general practitioner is not increasing much as most who experience the consequence of alcohol abuse will not seek treatment for minor ailments which is generally performed by general practitioners.

Markowitz et al. (2005) found "a negative and statistically significant relationship between the beer tax and male gonorrhoea rates" for the age groups of 15–19 and 20–24. They also found a negative and statistically significant effect of beer tax on the rates of AIDS. They made the point that the use of alcohol does not determine whether or not a teenager engages in sex, but the consumption of alcohol lowers the use of contraception. They suggest that gonorrhoea and AIDS may be reduced by increasing taxes on beer to reduce consumption. Of course, this conclusion may also be applied to any alcoholic beverage and illicit drugs once they have been legalized.

There are the direct cost of excessive alcohol consumption, such as extra healthcare costs, medical costs, costs of police and property damage. There are the indirect costs, such as the resulting costs because of productivity and losses of labour hours. There are also the non-financial welfare costs, such as costs of lives, pain and suffering.

The costs of alcohol abuse may also be compared with the costs of the abuse of other drugs; thus, various studies, for example, by Fenoglio et al. (2003) and Single et al. (1996), have shown that the cost involved in the excessive alcohol consumption exceeds or is similar to that of the usage of tobacco or other drugs.

Møller and Matic pointed to four types of costs that may be assessed in regard to the abuse of alcohol. The health cost resulting from the detrimental effect from alcohol abuse. There are also costs from crime resulting from the consumption of alcohol, including damage to property. There are the costs relating to the loss in productivity and labour resulting from lower productivity in the workplace and absenteeism and workers dying at an earlier age. There are also non-financial welfare costs which occur because of pain, suffering and loss of life.

Renna (2008) found that alcohol abuse reduces the number of hours worked and thereby lowers earnings of wages as a result of reduced earnings per hours worked as well as reduced numbers of hours worked. Renna (2008) argued that alcoholism had a greater detrimental effect on the labour market than alcohol abuse, both showed a negative coefficient in the numbers of hours of work which declined by the hours of annual work by 69 hours due to alcoholism. Alcoholism and alcohol abuse are not mutually exclusive but reinforce each other. Alcoholism was also shown to be higher in low-paying jobs than in other jobs.

The abuse of drugs declines the performance at work which may lead to greater staff turnover and a fall in remuneration and an increase in absenteeism and an increase in accidents. Drug abuse will also adversely affect cognitive functions, such as intellectual performance, which in turn will also adversely affect an individual's performance at work through hangovers, an increase in the number of sick days taken. As the drug abuse increases, the physiological and psychological consequences become more severe and reinforcing. It will also detrimentally affect the productivity of teamwork. Companies with difficulties amongst their staff with alcoholism could introduce various training programmes to promote better health amongst the staff and to increase workers' awareness of the detrimental effects of drug abuse; however, such programmes would have to be structured and long term and would require the cooperation of workers and trade unions to be effective.

Shahandeh (1985) argued that the common "image of the alcoholic as a 'derelict'" (p. 207) sharply contrasts with reality as the vast majority are actually employment. The abuse of alcohol and drugs has detrimental consequences at the workplace with wider repercussions for workers abusing alcohol and drugs, as well as for the family and co-workers with considerably social costs so that training programmes within companies may be beneficial for all those concerned.

Shahandeh (1985) made the point that the effects of drug and alcohol abuse in the workplace have become a considerable problem since the end of the 1940s; hence, the production of alcohol and its consumption and abuse has also spread quickly to workplaces. The abuse of alcohol may be caused by various psychological factors, such as the perceived need to overcome negative aspects caused by work which may cause stress, monotony and frustration, especially in lower class jobs, such as amongst blue-collar workers, for example, in the case of low wages, adverse labour-management relations, low job security and a hazardous work environment together with lack of career development as in industries which are dominated by mass production on assembly lines, for example, in the car industry, or long-distance truck drivers, pilots. Frustration is another cause of alcohol abuse, but frustration may be the result of failure which in itself may result from alcohol abuse so that alcohol abuse may reinforce frustration. Drugs are resorted to because of their short-term gratification that they may provide but have a detrimental effect in the long term which is caused because of the repetitive use of drugs which is another indication why the use of drugs has only short-term utility and therefore has no beneficial effect in the long term. Anything that is required to enhance an individual's performance in the long term is impeded in its efficacy so that drug abusers trade in long-term benefits for short-term gratifications. The associated social costs will increase the overall social costs so that there is essentially a welfare loss to the individual drug abuser as well as to society as a whole, both in terms of private and social costs which are sharply increasing at present.

There is a general acceptance that substance abuse is associated with accidents in the workplace; however, Feinauer (1990) contended that there is no evidence in support of this statement. He found in a review of the literature 31 authors who reported a relationship between accidents in the workplace and substance abuse without providing any firm evidence and their research design could not be evaluated (p. 15); however, this does not imply that there is no relationship between accidents in the workplace and drug abuse, rather their research design could not be evaluated. Neither does Feinauer (1990) provide any evidence that there is no relationship between accidents in the work place, decline in efficiency and abuse of alcohol.

Wagstaff (1987) argued that social cost estimates only show a partial picture of the costs and benefits to society as such estimates "ignore completely, for example, the private benefits of the activity" (p. 461) which are of course subsidized by the general public as they carry the burden of the social costs. He also argued that social cost estimates "provide no information on the costs of reducing social costs" (p. 461). In fact, he argued that in some cases, the cost prevention may be so great that it may not be in the public interests to pursue such government policies. Consumers may pay higher taxes on the drugs they consume and as their life expectancy is generally shorter, they also collect less old age pension; however, it is highly unlikely that in most cases, the social cost over a lifetime is negative as Wagstaff (1987) argued. In the case of forgone production when there is no compensation for loss of earnings in the case of sickness is being paid, then the user of drugs bears the full social cost and in the case of premature death, Wagstaff (1987) argued that this would most likely cause a net gain to third parties as the pension will not have to be paid. However, he overestimated the effect of a loss in productivity on wages because wages are generally rigid and do not readily adjust to levels of productivity.

The abuse of drugs also causes various other costs, for example, the costs involved in preventing future consumption and those involved in overcoming problems associated with previous consumption. Costs of legal enforcement may be regarded as being part of reducing future consumption, and costs incurred by, for example, voluntary organization in alleviating problems caused by past consumption of drugs. Wagstaff (1987) argued that "costs of reducing external costs ... are not external costs in themselves" (p. 463). Costs incurred to prevent future harm have to be compared with the benefits expected from the prevention of harm so that Wagstaff (1987) argued that such "benefits will take the form of a reduction in external costs" (p. 463). However, such costs which are incurred in reducing harm should be properly regarded as social costs because they would not have been incurred without the detrimental effects of drug abuse, whether in the form of nicotine, alcohol or any other drug. However, the costs involved in reducing external costs may be offset against the costs saved by reducing external costs. Any costs incurred in reducing social harm, and therefore social costs should be regarded as being part of external costs, even though they may reduce some of the external costs; what is relevant here is the net benefit as assessed through a cost–benefit analysis.

However, if social costs estimates are "highly questionable" (Wagstaff, 1987, p. 467), then this does not imply that policy decision makers should "ignore arguments for greater government action" in the area of drug abuse "which are based on social costs statistics" (p. 467), but rather that more research should be conducted to refine such statistics and knowledge about social costs have indeed widened since Wagstaff (1987) published his article.

Studies on social costs cannot indicate which policies are cost-effective, but they show the magnitude of the detrimental effects of alcohol abuse; however, cost–benefit analysis may show which policies are worthwhile to implement. Intangible costs turn non-monetary harm such as sufferings, into monetary value, some of such costs are carried by the abusers of alcohol themselves and some are carried by others.

Costs of substance abuse can be seen as opportunity costs which prevent resources from being used in other endeavours which can be referred to as opportunities forgone. However, the social and private costs of alcohol abuse are more difficult to assess because at low consumption of alcohol, it may not be harmful, whereas any use of tobacco is harmful to society so that it is easier to assess. An abuse of any drugs, including alcohol, as well as smoking will use more healthcare facilities than non-abusers. One way to measure the costs is to examine the excess admission rate of abusers above those of non-abusers.

Studies on the costs resulting from losses in productivity resulting from alcohol abuse may vary considerably because of the different approaches; for example, in a human capital approach, costs are multiple times greater than when using the friction cost approach. The human capital approach is often an overestimate as employees showing a slow productivity at work or die early because of alcohol abuse would be replaced in most situations so that the loss in productivity would not be permanent; whereas in the case of the friction cost approach, productivity loss may be an under-estimate because not all employee experiencing the effect of alcohol abuse will be replaced in the short term, depending on the prevailing economic conditions.

CHAPTER 8

Economic Remedies to Reduce Alcohol Abuse

Abstract This chapter will analyse the economic remedies to reduce alcohol abuse. The effectiveness of taxation policies depends to a large extent on the demand elasticities, such as own-price elasticity of demand, cross-price elasticity and aggregate price elasticity. The effect of minimum price policies on the abuse of alcohol will also be addressed. It is argued that a Pigovian tax on alcohol is justified because of the substantial costs such activities impose on society. A Pigovian tax can reduce the negative externalities which are created by such consumption and so can reduce market failure. A Pigovian tax on the consumption of alcohol may be regarded as being part of a public health policy to reduce the abuse of alcohol.

Keywords Elasticities of demand · excise tax – absorbed by producers · excise tax – passed on to consumers · Taxation policies · Price elasticities · Welfare theory · Pigovian tax · Minimum price policies

This chapter will analyse the economic remedies to reduce alcohol abuse. This chapter consists of three sections: (a) elasticities and the demand for alcohol, (b) taxation policies to reduce the abuse of alcohol and (c) minimum price policies and the abuse of alcohol.

Prices of alcoholic beverages have a considerable effect on drinking behaviour; for example, where to drink; so that bans on discounting or

J. Joshua, *The Economics of Addictive Behaviours Volume II*,
DOI 10.1007/978-3-319-54425-0_8

minimum pricing policies will also affect the consumption of alcohol. However, the effect on drinking behaviour varies with the pattern of drinking and with the categories of drinkers, such as the consumers' age or gender. Hence, a policy mix is called for when the aim is to reduce the prevalence of drinking.

Consumption taxes may come in various forms, for example, sales taxes and excise taxes may be levied on specific products, such as alcohol, tobacco products and gasoline. Excise duties are imposed to discourage consumption of products which are seen as detrimental to society, for example, when they contribute towards bad health or traffic congestions and thus may be referred to as sin taxes which can be earmarked for certain purposes, as in the case of providing medical care. The reliance on income tax imposes a burden on the general public, whereas excise duty is paid only by the user of the taxed product.

1 Elasticities and the Demand for Alcohol

The elasticity of demand for alcohol is the change in demand after a price change. If the elasticity is less than one, it is price inelastic, if it is greater than one, it is price elastic. Own-price elasticity of demand shows the change in quantity of a commodity demanded in response to changes in its own price. Own-price elasticity of demand is the percentage change in consumption resulting from a 1% change in price of that particular product.

If there are viable substitutions to a drug, then the cross-price elasticities also have to be considered. Cross-price elasticities show the response in switching consumption from various types of drugs, for example, how consumers switch between different products of alcohol. Cross-price elasticity of demand refers to different types of products, for example, in the case of alcoholic beverages, when the price of one product increases, consumers may switch to cheaper alternative alcoholic beverages.

Aggregate price elasticity refers to the overall price elasticity of demand for a group of products, such as alcohol. However, policies based on the aggregate price elasticity are inappropriate as the price elasticity of different alcoholic products vary widely. Demand is regarded as elastic when the proportional change in the quantity is greater than the proportional change in price, and it is inelastic if the proportional change in the quantity demanded is less than the proportional change in price. Demand curves have both elastic and an inelastic range so that the demand for a specific product may be elastic or inelastic over a certain range of quantity and price.

Meier et al. (2009, p. 387) found that in the United Kingdom, heavy alcohol consumers had higher own-price elasticities than moderate drinkers, but heavy alcohol consumers also had higher cross-price elasticities. However, even though they had higher own-price elasticities, this did not affect their alcohol consumption, but rather they switched to different alcoholic drinks (Meier et al., 2009, p. 387). In any design of an appropriate health policy regarding drug abuse, the participation elasticity is also of importance. The participation elasticity is the ratio of change in the number of drug users in response to a change in price, whereas the conditional elasticity is the ratio of change in the quantity of drugs used in response to a change in price.

Figure 8.1 shows the effects of an excise tax when absorbed by producer. SS and DD show the initial supply and demand curves and P_1 and Q_1 represent the price and quantity at the equilibrium. When an excise tax has been levied of an amount equal to P_2P_3, the supply curve will shift up by

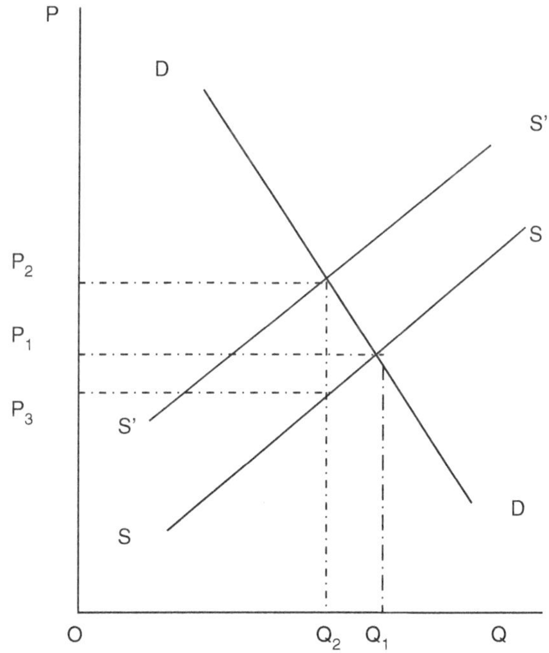

Fig. 8.1 Effects of an excise tax when absorbed by producer

the amount of the tax, so that the new supply curve will be S′S′ and so P_2 is the new price paid by consumers for Q_2 which is the quantity purchased.

However, an imposed excise tax may be passed on to the consumer so that in Fig. 8.1, the demand curve has shifted downwards by the amount equivalent of the imposed excise tax. P_2 then is the price paid by consumers which includes the imposed excise tax. The price which consumers pay when the tax is not passed on to the consumers is P_3 and Q_2 shows the commodity demanded after the imposition of the tax Fig. 8.2.

The effectiveness of taxation policies depends to a large extent on the demand elasticities. The elasticity of demand is the response to a change in price; that is, if an increase of 1% in price induces a greater change than 1% in consumption, then the good is price-elastic so that this will reduce consumption as well as expenditures on the price-elastic good. In the case of inelastic demand, the change in demand is less than the change in price so that an increase in price will also increase expenditures on the goods which are price-inelastic so that property crime may increase or users may increase their state of poverty.

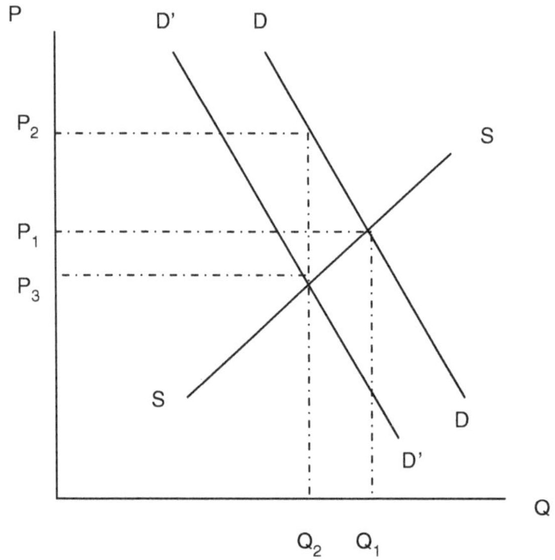

Fig. 8.2 Effects of an excise tax when passed on to consumers

The responsiveness to price may differ with the type of consumer and the condition under which the drug is consumed such as outlets, gender and age. Cross-price elasticities show how a change in the price of one drug will affect consumption of another drug, as users of drugs may switch to another drug when price of one drug increases. Parry and West (2004) showed that the optimal taxes on beer were higher than those of wine which were higher than those of spirits because demand for beer is comparatively inelastic, but demand for spirits is comparatively elastic.

Heavy drinkers are less price-sensitive compared to moderate drinkers, that is, –0.21 as compared with –.047 (see Gallet, 2007). However, as Meier et al. (2009) made the point, "heavy drinkers actually had higher own-price elasticities than moderate drinkers for most product categories" (p. 387), which is "counter-balanced by heavy drinkers also tending to have higher cross-elasticities which indicates more switching behaviour" (p. 387). Such switching behaviours will affect location of purchase, types of product and switches between products which are higher priced and lower priced products, whereby women are more sensitive to price changes than men. Meier et al. (2009) showed that "different drinking patterns are associated with different types of harm" (p. 389). Crime, disorder and absences from place of work were primarily associated with high alcohol intake during single drinking session, and crimes were related with drinking pattern of young drinkers, whereas most of the direct health cost as a result of drinking were associated with "long-term chronic drinking in older drinkers" (p. 390). Hence, the effect of the abuse of alcohol will depend on "what is consumed where, by whom and over what time-period" (p. 390). Abusers of alcohol are generally less responsive to price increases in alcohol because of their addiction.

As the consumption of alcohol can be addictive, the long-term price elasticity is larger than the short-term price elasticity (see Anderson and Baumberg, 2006). A negative own-price elasticity implies that changes in prices and consumption move in the opposite direction; that is, an increase in price will lower the consumption. If the consumption of alcoholic beverages is price-elastic, then the elasticity is greater than one so that the change in consumption is greater than the percentage change in price; for example, when the price elasticity is –1.5, then a 1% increase in the price of an alcoholic beverage will reduce the demand by 1.5%. On the other hand, price inelasticity implies that the proportional change in demand will be less than the proportional change in price. However, a Finnish study by Brunn et al. (1975) made the point that a decrease in the price of alcohol may have a greater effect on demand than an increase in the price by the same magnitude because of the addictive nature of alcohol.

Parry et al. (2006) agreed with numerous researchers that "beer should be taxed more heavily than wine on an alcohol equivalent basis, and that wine should be taxed more heavily than spirits" (p. 4); however, government policies generally do not concur with this as beer is generally taxed at a lower rate than wine or spirits. Furthermore, taxes on alcohol have declined in real terms; for example, taxes on alcohol in 2006 were 12% of pre-tax prices but were 50% in 1970 (Parry et al., 2006). It may appear that some governments try to keep the public sedated; the public is not interested in politics when they are intoxicated; so that the aim may be to keep the masses happy and contented, but it is not a viable health policy. Even though an increase in sales prices as a result of an imposed tax is quite effective, the real price of alcoholic beverages has decreased in many countries. Hence, excise taxes should be indexed annually for the consumer price index; otherwise, the sales price of alcoholic beverages will decline during times of inflation.

Taxation policies may change the prices of alcoholic beverages by imposing an excise tax which is based on the quantity of the consumption of alcohol, or a sales tax may be used which is based on the top of the price of the alcoholic beverage. The effects of the imposed excise tax will depend on how much of the excise tax is passed on to consumers or how much is absorbed by the alcohol industry. However, the rate of taxes, that is adjusted for inflation, has declined so that the real prices of alcoholic beverages have been reduced.

An increase in tax on the consumption of alcohol may be regarded as being part of a public health policy to reduce the abuse of alcohol and related consequences. However, taxes on alcohol may not be fully or even partially passed on to the consumer but instead may be absorbed by the retailer. Kenkel (2005) in his study of alcohol tax hikes in Alaska found that taxes on alcohol "are more than fully passed through to beverage prices... and that the pass-through patterns are similar across most popular brands of beer, wine, and spirit" (p. 276).

Studies by Wagenaar et al. (2009) and Anderson et al. (2009) have shown that price increases in alcohol reduces consumption and with it the detrimental effects of alcohol consumption. However, the real prices of alcohol and cigarettes, that is, after accounting for the rate of inflation, have declined significantly between 1951 and 1992 (Grossman et al.

1993). Over the last 50 years, the relative price of alcohol has decreased while at the same time, alcohol control measures have been liberalized so that the consumption of alcohol has increased and consequently alcohol related diseases have increased as well.

The imposition of an excise tax on alcoholic beverages certainly can save lives. According to Saffer and Grossman (1987b), if the federal excise tax would have been indexed to the inflation rate since 1951, 1,022 young lives aged between 18 and 20 could have been saved in a typical year in the period between 1975 and 1981 (Saffer and Grossman, 1987b). A beer tax of this order would have saved about 1660 lives per year between 1982 and 1988, and 5,000 lives could have been saved across all age groups (Chaloupka et al. 1993). An increase in the rate of tax on the consumption of alcohol would also reduce the overall rate of industrial accidents, of crime and of the number of working days lost.

In this case, alcoholics will gain when an increase in excise tax will reduce their consumption of alcohol; for example, Saffer and Grossman (1987a, b) found that excise taxes on alcohol reduce youth motor vehicle death rates, and Cook and Tauchen (1982) found that taxes on alcohol reduce heavy drinking together with the detrimental effects. Similarly, Phelps (1988) found that an increase in taxes on beer will reduce the consumption of beer by youth, and consequently the death rate resulting from road accidents, when 20% in tax increase caused a 33% decline in the death rate on roads, and a 30% tax increase caused a 40% decline in the death rate on roads. Phelps (1988) concluded that six or more drinks increase by 100-fold the risk of fatal motor vehicle accidents. Hence, an increase in excise taxes on alcohol is one of the cheapest and effective methods to save lives. He argued that an optimal tax rate on alcohol may be difficult to achieve, but an excise tax within the range of 25–40% is the second-best solution.

However, this ignores the substitution effect; that is, if youth switch to other alcoholic beverages after a tax increase in beer, then the road fatality may not decline as much as has been anticipated by Phelps (1988), but it still would be expected to decline to some extent. An excise tax would have to be placed on other alcoholic consumption because road accident fatalities is the result of all alcohol abuse so that the optimal rate of excise tax will differ if all alcohol consumption is considered, not just the consumption of beer.

Alcohol abuse similarly to the use of cigarettes and taxes on unhealthy foods to encounter obesity could be dealt with in a similar fashion; in this case, the leisure cross-price elasticities will have to be assessed to establish an optimal tax. When there are strong cross-price effects amongst beer, wine and spirits, there is a good case for the imposition of different tax on individual beverages based on the equivalent alcohol content. The elasticities of the demand of preferred alcoholic beverages are less than in the case of less preferred alcoholic beverages.

In the case of addictive goods, current consumption is related to past consumption so that consumers' response to an increase in excise taxes will increase over time. Thus, an increase in tax on alcoholic beverages may decrease consumption in the current as well in the following years, provided the rate of tax is not lowered again. Becker et al. (1991) and Becker (1992) made the point that the long-run price elasticity may increase with the level of addiction. Policies regarding adolescents are especially important as the abuse of drug is an addictive behaviour which often begins early in life. Mullahy and Sindelar (1990) argued that preventive policies which aim at preventing the onset of drug addiction might be most beneficial.

A focus on the younger age group in the prevention of alcohol abuse is also especially important because it is this age group that is mostly involved in fatal car accidents. Grossman et al. (1993) made the point that adolescents "are more sensitive to changes in money prices of addictive goods, whereas adults respond more to changes in the perceived or harmful consequences" (p. 215). There is considerable evidence in support of price sensitivity of youths; however, neither are adults always aware of the consequences of drug abuse; in any case, the consequences lie into the distant future. However, in the case of hyperbolic discounting, discounting may not undervalue the costs of their addiction occurring in the future.

Heavy and young drinkers consume generally cheaper alcohol which is widely available. To substantially increase excise taxes on alcohol will reduce consumption of alcohol, especially in high-risk groups which will also reduce the probability of young drinkers to take up drinking, and it reduces the probability of moderate consumers of alcohol to evolve into heavy drinkers (Anderson et al., 2009). Coate and Grossman (1988) and Kenkel (1993) found that the frequency and incidence of heavy alcohol consumption were inversely related to the price of alcohol.

2 Taxation Policies to Reduce the Abuse of Alcohol

The main way to increase alcohol prices is through taxation with the assumption that such taxes will be passed on to consumers by any increase in price. However, such taxes are often not passed on but instead are absorbed by the company as has been well illustrated by Ally et al. (2014) so that the effectiveness of an alcohol tax to reduce the harm caused by the consumption of alcohol depends largely on whether and by how much such taxes are passed on to the consumer. They found considerable difference in the tax being passed through in the case of cheaper and more expensive products. They also found considerable under-shifting in the case of the cheapest products while there was over-shifting in the case of products with an above median price, that is, price increased in the case of the cheaper products by less than the duty increased (under-shifting) while in the case of the more expensive products, there was considerable over-shifting, that is, prices increased by more than the imposed duty. Under-shifting is greatest in the case of beer. They found that 67% of total beer sales and 38% of total spirit sales were affected by under-shifting. Hence, this will reduce the effectiveness of taxation policy because high-risk abusers of alcohol favour cheaper alcohol and under-shifting will cause consumption to decline less than expected. Hence, the use of a minimum unit price (MUP) policy would be more effective in reducing the harmful consequences of alcohol consumption; it would also reduce the differences in harm from the consumption of alcohol between socio-economic groups. Nevertheless, taxation has become the policy mostly used to reduce the consumption of alcohol (Kenkel, 1996). However, the association between price increases through an increase in tax will depend on the price elasticity.

However, Black et al. (2010) found "that hazardous and harmful drinkers have little 'room' for elasticity as they already purchase their alcohol at very low prices, and indeed shop around to do so" (p. 735) so that the "harmed drinkers were already drinking as cheaply as they could" (p. 735). In the case of minimum pricing, the cheapest brand of cider would cost the same as the cheapest of lager so that there would be no incentive to switch to another product.

Black et al. (2010) also argued that the elimination of the cheapest alcoholic beverages through a minimum price policy may reduce their consumption. Over one-fifth of European adults admit to binge drinking, in Scotland over one quarter drink alcohol at a hazardous level. In England, over one-quarter drink alcohol at a hazardous level. The real price of alcohol has declined almost 70% in the United Kingdom since 1980 (Groves, 2010). Nutt et al. (2010) referred to alcohol as the most harmful substance in the United Kingdom. A policy of MUP of alcohol is aimed at reducing the cheapest alcoholic beverages which cause the greatest private and social harm caused mostly by hazardous drinkers.

Owang and Cho (2009) showed through their panel regression for Canada for the period from 1981 to 2004 that the estimated own-price elasticities indicated the effectiveness of taxation policy in reducing the consumption of spirits but were less effective in reducing the consumption of beer and wine. However, the cross-price elasticity estimates showed that levying a tax on beer or spirit was not effective in reducing consumers' demand of alcohol as they switched from beer or spirits to wine. They found a "positive and significant cross-price elasticity of demand for spirits with respect to the price of wine" (p. 609) so that "spirits may be a good substitute to wine" (p. 609). They found a "negative and significant cross-price elasticity of demand for spirits with respect to the price of beer" so that spirits may be a complement to beer. They also found a positive and significant cross-price elasticity of demand for beer with respect to the price of wine so that beer is a substitute for wine.

Stockwell et al. (2011) concluded that increases in minimum prices of alcohol beverages are able to reduce the consumption of alcohol. Canada is one of the few countries which have introduced a minimum price of alcohol policy. A combination of a tax policy and a minimum price policy is likely to be even more effective in reducing the abuse of alcohol than an imposition of a tax alone. The heavier drinkers have a preference for the cheapest priced drinks so that minimum price policies on alcoholic drinks are able to reduce the hazards of alcohol abuse, more than any other policies it targets mostly the hazardous drinkers. They found that a 10% increase in the minimum price of an alcoholic beverage reduces its demand by between 14.6% and 16.1%. Of course, their results are based on legally sold alcohol and do not make any allowance for home-made alcoholic drinks or which have been purchased on the black market, but this is unlikely to invalidate their research as home-made alcoholic drinks would be a relatively small proportion of the total alcohol consumed.

The effects of a tax on alcoholic beverages are often mitigated by retailers selling alcohol at heavily discounted prices and other promotional schemes. A minimum price per unit of alcohol policy would be able to overcome largely this problem. A minimum price policy on alcohol will be most beneficial to hazardous drinkers as it will have a beneficial effect on their health, even though they will pay a substantial higher price for their consumption of alcohol. It is these hazardous drinkers that present the greatest risk to themselves and to the community at large so that their drinking behaviour requires positive intervention to reduce the harm from the abuse of alcohol.

Much of the alcohol-related costs are the huge external costs which are not considered when consumers make their decisions to purchase alcohol. An imposed tax on alcohol may be used to correct this market failure. However, the effectiveness of any tax policy will depend on individuals' responsiveness to changes in the price of different alcoholic beverages.

Various epidemiologists and other health professionals such as Klatsky et al. (1990) and McGregor et al. (2003) have studied the association between demographic and personal characteristics and the consumption of different types of alcohol. The heterogeneity of the consumption of alcohol provides important information to enable an assessment of the effect of minimum price and tax policies regarding the consumption of alcohol and their effects on health so that policies can be more effectively targeted.

Ramful and Zhao (2008) estimated the own-price elasticities of the consumption of beer, wine and spirit at -0.95, -1.85 and -0.73, respectively so that the consumption of wine is highly responsive to its own price. They also showed that the consumption of different types of alcoholic products relate to different groups of population. Hence, price policies have to take such differences into account if such policies are to be effective. They found that the own and cross-price elasticities are different for the general population as compared to subpopulations, which is another important consideration to be taken into account when designing appropriate policies on the consumption of alcohol.

Generally, the higher the price of alcohol, the lower is the demand so that there is an inverse relationship between the prices of alcohol and the consumption of alcohol. Taxation imposed on alcohol is a main policy instrument to increase the price of alcohol; however, in the United States, the real tax rates on alcoholic beverages have declined since 1951 (Xu and Chaloupka, 2011). The demand for alcoholic beverages is more responsive to price changes in the long run rather than in the short run; for example, Gallet (2007) found through a meta-analysis of elasticities that the median price elasticities for all alcoholic beverages were -0.52 in the short run and -0.82 in the long run.

Policies to regulate the market of alcohol are highly effective in reducing the harm caused by the abuse of alcohol. Excise taxes are especially successful in reducing the harm of alcohol abuse of young people; for example, an increase of the price of alcohol by 10% in the EU would save more than 9,000 lives in the following year while approximately €13 billion of additional revenue due to the increase in the excise taxes would be collected (Anderson and Baumberg, 2006, p. 7).

Net revenue from taxes on alcohol can be increased by a moderate increase in the tax on alcohol even though overall consumption of alcohol declines. Costs related to the abuse of alcohol include costs of treatment of alcohol-related problems, costs for the social welfare system and the criminal justice system. Excise taxes in terms of government revenue collected are not a benefit to society, but rather they are transfer payments. As the consumption of alcohol is relatively inelastic, tax revenue collected by the government depends mainly on the level of tax rather than the level of consumption.

The raising of tax on alcohol is cost-effective. The collection of higher taxes does not require more resources than the collection of lower taxes, and the effect of a tax on alcohol is effective in reducing demand for alcohol, although an increase in tax on the consumption of alcohol will reduce the consumption depending on various elasticities as outlined above. However, rates of tax may be so high that it encourages the smuggling of alcoholic beverages into the country or the unrecorded consumption, which is generally home-made, or the illicit production of alcohol; as such, it is not taxed and it is outside of government control as it is produced, distributed and sold outside of the usual channels of trading. Although the introduction of an appropriate taxation policy has a low cost of implementation, there is the problem of possible avoidance of paying such an imposed tax. Furthermore, a high rate of dependence may make a policy less effective because consumers who are dependent on alcohol may feel a compulsive need for alcohol and are therefore less affected by the price, unless there is a substantial increase in the price.

Besides the imposition of tax on alcoholic beverages, pricing policies are also effective in reducing the consumption of alcohol. Restrictions could be placed on minimum sales prices or of discounted sales. Fixing MUPs for alcohol can be supplemented with excise taxes on alcohol. A minimum price system would increase the retail price of the cheapest form of alcoholic beverages. While an excise tax could be absorbed by the manufacturer, the effect of a minimum price system cannot be reduced by the producers or wholesalers. To reduce the maximum trading hours and reducing the density of outlets will reduce purchases of alcoholic beverages and consequently the associated detrimental effect of alcohol consumption.

An increase in prices of alcohol may reduce the consumption of alcohol; however, consumers may switch to other drugs, such as marijuana. Pacula (1998) found that alcohol and marijuana were complements so that they are used together. In this case, an increase in the tax of alcohol would not only reduce the demand for alcohol but also for marijuana. However, other studies, such as by Chaloupka and Laixuthai (1997), found that an increase in price in one will shift demand to the substitute commodity. This could also imply that when marijuana is decriminalized, there may be a shift to marijuana away from beer, especially when a tax is placed on the consumption of beer; on the other hand, a higher price in marijuana may shift demand on to beer. A reduction of demand for alcohol because of the imposition of an excise tax would reduce employment in the alcohol industry; however, most workers who lose their jobs in the alcohol industry would find employment in other industries so that the loss in employment would be in most cases only frictional unemployment in the short term, unless the economy is experiencing a fall in general employment due to a recession.

Durrance et al. (2011) found that an increase in taxes on alcohol will reduce the consumption of alcohol but did not find that a reduction in alcohol consumption will also reduce female homicide. Similarly, Averett and Wang (2016) concluded that there is no evidence that lower prices of alcohol will reduce intimate violence between intimate partners. Nevertheless, it is well known that a reduction of the availability of alcoholic beverages and a decline in their prices will also reduce the detrimental effect of alcohol abuse.

Wagenaar et al. (2009) using a meta-analysis from 112 studies found that changes in price affect all kinds of beverages and all kinds of consumers whether light or heavy drinkers; however, it affected the drinking behaviour of heavy drinkers less than that of other drinkers. The demand of alcoholic beverages also fluctuates with consumers' affordability (Rabinovich et al., 2009). While income in most EU countries has increased between 1966 and 2004, prices of alcoholic beverages have either relatively declined or have remained stable (Rabinovich et al., 2009).

The poorer section of the community would spend proportionately more of their income on excise tax than those in higher income brackets so that an excise tax in this case is regarded by many economists as regressive; however, as an increase of tax will reduce the consumption of alcohol, it will have a considerable beneficial effect on health; hence, the poorer section of the community may gain more of the beneficial health effect; this is especially the case as the poorer section of the community do consume a greater quantity of alcohol so that the detrimental effects of the consumption of alcohol are considerably greater for the poorer communities; however, such detrimental effect of alcohol consumption would then be reduced by an increase in tax as it reduces consumption.

Furthermore, to impose tax on the value of alcohol is less regressive because higher income earners tend to buy more expensive wine, whereas imposing an alcohol tax based on the quantity of alcohol would more likely reduce externalities. It is also the case that lower income earners are often less responsible in the consumption of alcohol; hence, an increase in taxes on the content of alcohol will be more effective in reducing the detrimental effects of alcohol abuse.

As alcoholism is a disease, consumers who suffer from alcoholism have a negative consumer surplus so that their consumption of alcohol cannot be welfare maximizing or welfare enhancing; hence, consumers who are alcoholics will benefit if they reduce their consumption of alcohol. Pogue and Sgontz (1989) argued that the average tax rate on alcohol should be significantly increased if the abuse of alcohol is a disease. Abusers of alcohol lose utility per unit of alcohol consumed rather than gaining utility when consuming alcohol so that an increase in excise tax on alcohol will increase their utility. Taxes may be imposed in order to minimize welfare losses rather than just to cover the costs of externalities.

Fogarty (2011) has illustrated that a tax rate on alcohol will vary considerably with the type of alcoholic beverage consumed if such a tax is to balance the costs imposed on moderate drinkers against the welfare gains by lowering costs of externalities. Fogarty (2011) argued that this tax approach would also balance more the interests of the wider community with those of the manufacturer of the alcoholic beverages as the optimal tax declines when either the share of the abusive consumption declines or the share of the uninformed abusers declines. The uninformed abusers are those who do not know the costs associated with their abusive consumption. Richardson and Crawley (1994) also showed that tax rates can be set so that they cover external costs and so can increase the gain in welfare.

As the response by consumers to price changes will differ between types of alcoholic beverages, community welfare will be maximized by setting specific tax rates for each specific alcoholic beverage per litre of pure alcohol. Prices of alcoholic beverages depend on the type as well as the quality of the product and the outlet of sales. Much research has been done on the effect of excise taxes on alcoholic beverages generally; an increase in the excise tax will increase the sales price and reduce the consumption of alcohol and thereby reduces the detrimental effect of the consumption of alcohol. However, prices may also be changed.

It may be argued that taxes on smoking and alcohol consumption should be related to the external costs caused by smokers and alcohol abusers. However, different writers have disagreed on whether a tax on the consumption of alcohol is appropriate to cover or to reduce social costs. The social costs of alcohol consumption are considerable so that some writers argued for a substantial excise tax on the consumption of alcohol. Others argue that a tax imposed on the consumption of alcohol would affect consumers of alcohol indiscriminately whether they are abusers of alcohol or not. A tax may not reduce the social costs as it is caused mainly by those who abuse alcohol. If alcoholism is a behavioural disease, then the consumer surplus of alcoholics may be negative. According to welfare theory, it is argued that consumers of alcohol enjoy a net benefit which is the "consumer surplus"; however, alcoholics over-consume due to their addiction so that consumer surplus from their marginal consumption is negative. As alcoholism is regarded here as a disease, alcoholics will benefit from ceasing the abuse of alcohol. Alcoholics will gain when taxes on the consumption of alcohol will reduce their consumption because of a reduction in internal abuse costs. To assess the optimal tax rate for a particular alcoholic beverage, tax on substitute beverages has also to be considered. If tax is imposed on one beverage without imposing a tax on substitute beverages, there may be a substitution away from the taxed beverage to the untaxed beverage.

An increase in prices of alcoholic beverages has been found to be successful in reducing demand in low-income countries, such as in China (Pan et al., 2006) and in South Africa (Parry et al., 2003) and in high-income countries, such as in Australia (Gallet, 2007; see also Wagenaar et al., 2009). However, Anderson and Baumberg (2006) made the point that taxes on the consumption of alcohol are below the social costs that are created through the consumption of alcohol.

It may be argued that a Pigovian tax on alcohol, cigarettes, legal drugs and soft drinks is justified because of the substantial costs such activities impose on society. A Pigovian tax can reduce the negative externalities which are created by such consumption and so can reduce market failure. A Pigovian tax may be imposed according to the level of alcoholic content in beer, liquor and wine.

The effect of an imposition of an alcohol tax, Pigovian or otherwise, will also depend on the structure of the industry. Within a highly competitive environment, tax may be difficult to be passed on to the consumers, whereas within a non-competitive environment, the company may pass on the tax. Most companies involved in the production and distribution of cigarettes, alcohol or other drugs are oligopolies and therefore are likely to pass on the tax to the consumer. Of course, legislations could require that consumers have to pay any such tax imposed.

The Pigovian tax is equal, for example, to the weighted sum of the marginal external cost of drunk driving minus the pecuniary penalty resulting from drunk driving. The weights are derived from the elasticities of drunk driving and heavy drinking with respect to the prices of alcohol relative to the own-price elasticity of alcohol (see Parry and West, 2004, p. 13). Parry et al. (2006) showed that the welfare gains deriving from an alcohol tax "are decoupled from the level of non-pecuniary penalties when changes in the first-order deadweight losses associated with these penalties are taken into consideration" (p. 4). To reduce road fatalities due to drunk driving requires the imposition of an optimal tax on alcohol as well as harsher penalties for drunk driving to such an extent that it would be politically untenable.

As the smoking of cigarettes is detrimental at any level, the implementation of a tax policy is straight forward. The situation is more complex with a tax imposed on the consumption of alcohol as it will not distinguish between moderate consumption of alcohol and the abuse of alcohol. To drink alcohol at a low level will not endanger one's health. The detrimental effect of alcohol consumption begins with the heavy use and abuse of alcohol. The use of alcohol and cigarettes starts mostly during the adolescent years and can become addictive. Hence, Mullahy and Sindelar (1993) argued that a viable policy may be to prevent the initiation of the use of alcohol and cigarettes. An increase in the rate of tax on the consumption of alcohol will reduce morbidity and mortality (see Grossman et al., 1993; Cook and Moore, 2002).

Cook and Moore (1994) made the point that when in the United States, 29 states lowered the drinking age, it led to a sharp increase in traffic fatalities, whereas, when the states mandated in 1984 that all states ban the sales of alcoholic beverages to anyone under the age of 21, the traffic fatalities sharply declined. However, the effectiveness of the taxes declined over the years because of the rate of inflation during the 1970s and 1980s. Higher prices of alcoholic beverages through the imposition of an excise tax will reduce alcohol abuse and the associated private and social costs (Cook and Moore, 1994).

Taxes on alcoholic beverages have to remain effective. However, as Cook and Moore explained, there were no increases in the rate of tax on alcoholic beverages between 1951 and 1990 so that the tax rate declined, so that relative prices of alcoholic beverages have declined, so that the ratio of alcoholic beverages prices to the CPI declined by 28% between 1967 and 1982 and liquor prices decreased by 50% (Cook, and Moore, 1993). The proposition that consumers of alcoholic beverages should pay for the full social costs which are caused through their drinking behaviour can be articulated in terms of efficiency as well as fairness.

Heavy drinkers use a disproportionate share of government expenditures on healthcare, criminal justice system as well as long-term care so that tax on alcoholic beverages may be regarded as user pay fees. To strengthen the argument about fairness, it may be argued that it may be argued that extra revenue is to be used to compensate victims of alcohol abuse. An increase in taxes on alcoholic beverages also would lead towards a decline in the consumption of alcoholic beverages which also would decline the social costs caused by the consumption of alcohol. As heavy drinkers use a disproportionate share of government expenditures on medical expenditures, it may be argued that they also should pay towards such expenses a greater share. As many of the victims of alcohol abuse are blameless, it is even more important that they shall be compensated for the damage which has been inflicted on them.

A Pigovian tax may be used to increase the price to the level which includes the social costs. Pogue and Sgontz (1989) estimated that in 1989, the actual excise taxes were approximately 50% of the final level of social costs. However, as Pogue and Sgontz (1989) argued, alcohol is for many consumers of alcohol a complement to leisure. If it is argued that leisure is under-priced, then an imposition of taxes on products which are complements to leisure and substitutes for investment in human capital may be imposed. Hence, Cook and Moore (1993) argued that special alcohol taxes could be justified to reduce the demand for alcohol as the supply of alcohol is too easily available. Such a special tax on alcohol would serve as a corrective device for incentive problems which are caused by other taxes and so may increase efficiency. It may be argued that the death rate for innocent victims, which are those who were not intoxicated at the time of the vehicle crash, may be more relevant in order to establish an appropriate tax rate. Cook and Moore (1993) estimated that "one-third of the victims of drunk drivers were not intoxicated".

As alcoholism is a disease, it can be argued that alcoholics over consume because their consumer surplus from marginal from their marginal consumption is zero or even negative. Costs of alcohol abuse may be carried by the abuser; in that case, they are internal costs and other costs may be imposed on others so that they are referred to as external costs, such as injury to others and damage to property. Many economists assume that consumers are well informed so that their decisions are welfare maximizing. However, as alcoholism is a disease, the decision to abuse alcohol cannot be assumed to be welfare maximizing; hence, alcoholics do not benefit from their abuse of alcohol but instead benefit by a reduction in their consumption of alcohol which can be achieved partly through an imposition of an excise tax on alcoholic beverages so that an increase in tax may serve to benefit abusers of alcohol. Hence, alcoholics will gain when an imposition of taxes on alcoholic beverages will reduce their abuse of alcohol.

In the case of alcoholics, consumer surplus from the gained consumption of alcohol is negative so that a tax on alcoholic beverages will increase the welfare of alcohol abusers which is caused by a decrease in internal costs, such as medical costs resulting from alcohol abuse. The general standard consumer choice cannot be applied to the abuse of alcohol because information about the alcohol market is imperfect as alcohol abusers are generally addicted to their consumption of alcohol (see Becker, Grossman, and Murphy, 1987).

The imposition of an excise tax on the consumption of alcohol may reduce mortality as it reduces the consumption of alcohol. However, a meta-analysis conducted by Rehm et al. (2001) found that the rate of death increased for men under the age of 45 with an increase of alcohol consumption, but for men over 45 years of age, the mortality follows a J-shaped curve.

3 Minimum Price Policies and the Abuse of Alcohol

Scotland was the first country which introduced in 2012 a MUP policy for alcoholic beverages, although it has been challenged by alcohol manufacturers as it interferes with European Laws. After years of resistance by the UK government to introduce such a policy, they now advocate a price of 40 pence per unit as a minimum price (The Home Office, 2012) and also intend to ban sales of "below cost". When Denmark joined the EU, it began to lower its taxes on alcohol along with EU regulations so that consequently the consumption of alcohol increased significantly and consequently the harm derived from the consumption of alcohol increased as well.

However, price interventions that are aimed at heavier drinkers of alcohol are more effective in reducing the consumption of alcohol and consequently the harm caused by the misuse of alcohol. Minimum unit pricing or floor price targets those who are at the greatest risk of harm, that is, the heaviest drinkers on lower incomes so that the policies have the greatest beneficial effect on this group as well as it reduces their alcohol consumption and consequently the detrimental effects on their health and thereby would reduce the inequalities in health between the different income groups.

A MUP for alcohol and a uniform volumetric tax would have only a slight effect on consumption of light and moderate consumers; however, it would have a greater impact on the consumption by heavy drinkers without having much effect on moderate drinkers. Hence, MUP and a uniform volumetric tax would reduce the overall social costs and the detrimental effect on health caused by heavy drinkers. Hence, MUP and a uniform volumetric tax would reduce the overall social costs and the detrimental effect on health caused by heavy drinkers. Market failure provides a rational for intervention in pricing; for example, by including the social costs in the price; although it may be difficult in some situations to assess the appropriate adjustment to the price. However, there is a significant negative association caused by the misuse of alcohol death and minimum prices of alcohol.

A minimum price policy will affect those who will buy cheaper products and heavy drinkers are also likely to buy mostly cheap alcoholic beverages, whereas a general increase in excise taxes on alcohol would affect all consumers as it would be placed equally on all products. Hence, a minimum price policy has a greater beneficial impact on society by reducing overall social costs as it would be directed more towards the heaviest drinkers. The argument that a minimum price policy would be regressive becomes largely irrelevant as the health of heavy drinkers would also benefit to a larger extent. Much of the extra revenue collected from a minimum price policy may also be used to compensate the industry for lower sales, but it may be more appropriate to use such revenue to compensate for the social costs which is caused through the abuse of alcohol.

A MUP for alcohol may prevent consumers to downshift or to substitute to a cheaper product. Heavy drinkers do respond to price increases by switching to cheaper products. As they maintain their alcohol intake, the impact of a price increase is partly minimized. On the other hand, the imposition of a minimum price based on a uniform price per unit of alcohol could mitigate this substitution effect. Wagenaar et al. (2009) found in their meta-analysis that price elasticities between countries for different products vary in regard to the consumption of alcohol varies.

A minimum price policy has advantages over a general tax on alcohol. Taxes can be absorbed and they are not aimed at reducing the consumption of heavy drinkers and thus do not reduce the harm caused by heavy drinkers to themselves and to others. On the other hand, a minimum pricing policy is a more refined policy as it can address better the problems caused by heavy drinkers.

Decisions should be guided by the empirical evidence that is available when introducing policies rather than decided by misinformed ideologies which overrides science to serve vested interests. Meier et al. (2009) made policy proposals based on empirical evidence regarding the regulation of prices of alcohol. Their results confirm numerous studies even though their research could be further strengthened with more longitudinal studies. The most important point of their studies is that the average price paid per unit of alcohol declines with the number of drinks consumed so that heavy drinkers also occur the greatest harm resulting from their alcohol consumption. As heavy drinkers are more own-price responsive as well as more cross-price responsive, they are likely to reduce their alcohol consumption by more than do moderate drinkers, when the price of their preferred alcoholic beverages increases. They are also more likely to switch to another lower-priced alcoholic brand. A minimum price policy would largely prevent this. A minimum price policy will also reduce price competition. An optimum price policy regarding alcohol would combine an increase in base tax rates with a minimum price policy. Wagenaar et al. (2009) provided evidence through their meta-analysis that the price mechanism can be highly effective in reducing the consumption of alcohol. Prices can be changed through the imposition of excise taxes or through the setting of minimum prices, but a combination of such policies would be more effective in reducing the abuse of alcohol.

CHAPTER 9

The Politics of Corporate and Social Responsibilities

Abstract This chapter will address the politics of corporate and social responsibilities. The alcohol industry emphasizes self-regulation and rejects marketing regulations; instead, the industry argues that the consumption of alcohol is a matter of free choice made by the consumer. The industry also rejects health warnings as not all users of alcohol are abusers of alcohol. Instead, the concept of social marketing may be used as an alternative concept to marketing. The concept of social marketing can be applied to the marketing of products which have a detrimental impact on the consumers' health. Products may have to be checked for their propensity to create ill health before they can be sold on the market. The aim of social marketing is to facilitate change in adverse behaviour.

Keywords Corporate social responsibilities · Corporate responsibilities and social costs

This chapter will address the politics of corporate and social responsibilities. This chapter is divided in two sections: (a) corporate social responsibilities and policies, and (b) corporate responsibilities and social costs.

J. Joshua, *The Economics of Addictive Behaviours Volume II*,
DOI 10.1007/978-3-319-54425-0_9

1 Corporate Social Responsibilities and Policies

The alcohol industry emphasizes self-regulation by the industry and rejects marketing regulations; instead, the industry argues that the consumption of alcohol is a matter of free choice made by the consumer. The industry also rejects health warnings as not all users of alcohol are abusers of alcohol. Many countries prevent the advertising of tobacco products and as the social as well as the private costs as a result of alcohol abuse are substantial, there may be good reasons to ban advertisements of alcoholic beverages as well.

The alcohol industry rejects marketing regulation and instead emphasizes industry responsibility and argues instead that self-regulation is more effective than statutory regulation and instead emphasizes individual responsibility. However, to include themes of responsible use of alcohol in the advertisements of alcoholic beverages is meant to increase sales and has little to do with social responsibility but instead intends to promote a public image of being socially responsible. The alcohol industry argues that regulations of advertising and trade restrictions interfere with international trade and international agreements on investments and thereby attempts to shift away from issues of consumer protection and public health.

Regulations are seen by the alcohol industry and others as interfering with individual's choices; however, the promotion of products through advertising is there to manipulate people's choices in the first place. Furthermore, there is a lack of evidence to show that self-regulation reduces the detrimental effects of the abuse of alcohol consumption. In contrast to the alcohol industry's claim, marketing does change people's consumption and behaviour. Through marketing, adolescents become drawn into the culture of drinking alcohol, first by being initiated into the use of alcohol and then by becoming a life-long consumer of alcohol. Indeed, much of advertising is created to appeal to adolescents who are below the legal minimum age of drinking but who provide then the future profits for the company.

The marketing by the alcohol industry greatly influences the consumption of alcohol by affecting the initiation into the use of alcohol, and its prevalence and pattern of the consumption of alcohol. Savell et al. (2016) made the valid point that the alcohol industry attempts to shift the blame for the misuse of alcohol to the consumer and argued for responsible consumption through education. Such themes are often to some extent included in the advertisements of alcoholic beverages to enhance the public image of the corporation, although the overriding aim of advertising is the promotion of their product. The alcohol industry argues against population-level approaches to reduce the consumption of alcohol as it, according to the alcohol industry, unduly penalizes moderate drinkers, which as Savell et al. (2016) argued has the potential to undermine any focus on health policies. The alcohol industry also opposes health warnings because alcoholic beverages are not like cigarettes as alcohol can be consumed in moderation without causing any harm. However, health warnings may give some consumers the incentives to drink in moderation.

As governments often consult with the tobacco or alcohol industry before passing legislations, this can lead to watered-down ineffective legislations as such companies are mainly concerned with sustaining their profitability so that legislations of this kind usually lead to compromises at the cost of the health of the public. Alcohol and tobacco policies are subject to competing interests and ideologies.

Kotler and Roberto (1989) developed the concept of social marketing as an alternative concept to marketing as it is generally understood, or even as an alternative to corporate social responsibility. The concept of social marketing can be applied to the marketing of products which have a detrimental impact on the consumer's health. The aim of social marketing is to facilitate change in adverse behaviour. Applied to alcohol abuse, it may be able to induce abusers of alcohol and thereby also reduces the undesirable social and thereby also reduces the undesirable social costs which are caused by the abuse of alcohol. Marketing strategies may aim at product substitution. Social marketing will also have to consider the response to social techniques of marketing; for example, non-abusers of alcohol. Viable social marketing strategies also have to consider the background of the consumers such as personal characteristics and their demographics and lifestyle. Various strategies may be used to reduce the abuse of alcohol. Products may also have to be checked for their propensity to create illnesses and diseases before they can be sold on the market with the appropriate certificate, not just the increase of GDP but its effects on other parameters. Such procedures may also enhance their image if the product is certified as being faultless.

2 Corporate Responsibilities and Social Costs

Restrictions to reduce alcohol abuse may include the banning of or limiting the advertisements which promote the consumption of alcohol. However, the alcohol industry attempts to undermine any controls on the consumption of alcohol. Alcohol companies are using corporate social responsibilities as a public relation exercise and highlight consumer's individual responsibilities. The alcohol industry argues that individual responsibility is the best way to prevent alcohol-induced harms. However, self-regulations of the tobacco and alcohol industries have been largely unsuccessful so that new regulation may be required. Social responsibility messages by alcohol companies may have a beneficial impact on the reputation of the company but have little effect on public health. Such messages are conveyed through advertisements to increase sales whereby drinking alcohol is seen as "fun" which overwhelms any "responsibility" message there may be (Smith et al., 2006).

Alcohol companies advertise especially in media to which adolescents are exposed to; to encapsulate the market of the young will perpetuate the demand for alcoholic beverages into the future. There is a direct relationship between the advertising of tobacco products and alcoholic beverages and the size of the adolescent readership of a particular medium in the case of advertisements for beer and spirit, but this was not the case with wine (Garfield et al., 2003). Personalities who are being used on television to promote alcoholic beverages are usually well known, are often of high social status and usually are portrayed as being wealthy. Advertisements portray the drinking of alcohol as being full of fun associated with social activities within a relaxed and happy social atmosphere together with social achievement (Wallack et al., 1990; Grube, 1993). The advertisements of alcohol are embedded within a milieu that is appealing to adolescents using rock music, celebrity endorsers, sociability, physical attractiveness and animation (Grube, 1993; Aitken and Eadie, 1988, Aitken, 1989). The constant portrayals of incidental drinking create a belief with the wider public that drinking alcohol is a normal activity (Aitken and Eadie, 1988, Aitken, 1989) so that there is a good reason for such advertisements to be phased out.

The more young people will be exposed, the greater will be their consumption of alcohol. To reduce exposure, for example, through phasing out advertisements will reduce the initiation into drinking alcohol and also will reduce heavy drinking (World Health Organization, 2009b). As alcohol companies intend to increase their profits, their aim is to increase the volume of alcohol consumed and not as it is claimed by the industry, just to make consumers aware of a specific brand. Advertisements of alcoholic beverages also make it more difficult for heavy drinkers or problem drinkers to give up drinking alcohol as they are constantly reminded of the consumption of alcohol as being a normal activity (Thompson et al., 1997).

The New Zealand Medical Association (NZMA, 2015) has referred to the widely available and cheap alcohol together with sophisticated marketing, as an "alcogenic' environment" (p. 02). The NZMA (2015) stated that the evidence on which alcohol policies can be based are available; "where there are conflicts of interests between the public health of New Zealanders and the profits of private commercial entities, public health considerations should prevail" (p. 02). The NZMA (2015) advocated an increase in excise taxation on alcohol and advocated the introduction of a minimum unit pricing policy and argued that more of the revenue raised should be spend on alcohol "harm" reduction. The NZMA (2015) also advocated the phasing out of alcohol marketing through the appropriate legislations rather than through industry self-regulation, much of such advertisements are shown during sporting and cultural events and generally include sponsorships.

Unless much needed changes are enforced through legislations, sponsorships and advertisements during sport venues and advertisements in general are unlikely to be phased out. Furthermore, under a competitive system, costs have to be minimized and many of the required changes under self-regulation, if implemented, are costly; that is, corporations which alone introduce the required changes will be at a competitive disadvantage; hence, there is a conflict of interest between corporate interest and public health (see World Health Organization, 2012).

Other issues that are often raised are the effects on the economy, more specifically, the effect on employment in the case of a decline in demand of alcohol, and the relationship between public health and public finance when considering a tax on alcohol. In 1990, within the European Union of 12 members, only 2% of the total civilian work force was employed in the production of alcohol and trade, mostly within the retail sector. Only one quarter of it was involved in the production of alcoholic beverages (Lehto, 1997, p. S55), although it is higher in some regions.

Multinational corporations control much of people's lives. The top 100 companies owned 33% of the world assets (Wiist, 2010). The behavioural diseases of smoking, the consumption of alcohol and the habit of overeating are controlled by a few corporations, especially in the case of the tobacco industry and the fast food industry. Under neoliberal policies, corporations have increased their influence enormously. They advise governments and often become part of the government through the revolving door scheme as advisers and are engaged in forceful lobbying. In the United States and other western countries, many bankers and executives of multinational corporations have been or are part of the government or of international organizations which influence the political decision-making process. Corporations of the alcohol industry, the tobacco industry and the food industry have an enormous impact on public health policy and through such health policy will affect public health.

The production, distribution, marketing and consumption of alcohol create employment, provide income for producers and retailers and also provide government revenue through tax. However, the detrimental effect greatly outweighs the material benefits. The detrimental effects of the abuse of alcohol are caused through the physical toxicity, intoxication and alcohol dependence which are reinforced through sustained heavy drinking of alcohol. The repeated intoxication through the chronic drinking of alcohol leads to behavioural, physical and cognitive symptoms which reinforce each other to result in dependence.

Like in the case of fast food, soft drinks and cigarettes, the alcohol industry engages in vast advertisement campaigns to increase their sales and profits. The production and distribution of alcoholic beverages, tobacco products and fast food are part of the global economy; they collectively provide employment and wages at the production and distribution levels and they also provide tax revenues. However, such benefits are considerable less than the private and social costs that result from the usage of such products (see Chapter 4). Hence, there is a valid reason why the advertisements of such products should be prohibited or at the very least be curtailed.

As demand for alcohol declines, resources would move out of the alcohol industry and employment would follow; assuming there is no recession, employment opportunities may arise elsewhere so that in the longer term, the main costs would be transaction costs due to frictional unemployment. Furthermore, when the consumption of alcohol in Italy declined by 33% between 1980 and 1990, employment in restaurants, hotels and cafes increased by 24% (Lehto, 1997, p. S56) while employment in the agricultural and industrial sectors has declined; however, much of it was due to changes in technology of production; for example, while the consumption of alcohol in Ireland remained much the same, employment declined by 45% between 1981 and 1991 (Lehto, 1997, p. S56).

As consumption of alcohol has stabilized in developed countries, manufacturers of alcoholic beverages are moving into developing countries. There are policies and relevant laws to decrease the abuse of alcohol in developing countries, but such laws are often not well enforced. A national strategy to reduce the abuse of alcohol includes a legal framework and its enforcement. Voluntary constraints by the alcohol industry are not very effective but are often used as a public relation exercise, similarly, as within the tobacco and fast food industries. Decisions have to be based on scientific evidence rather than the advice of pressure groups, whereby the health of the nation should be the prime concern. Furthermore, the World Health Organization (2014) argued that “the alcohol industry has no role in the formulation of alcoholic policies” (p. 24).

Barbor et al. (2013) made the point that despite the enormous hardship through the epidemics which have been caused by alcohol abuse, over-eating and smoking, it will take decades before more health conscious policies will be adopted.

CHAPTER 10

Conclusion

Abstract This second volume of the economics of addictive behaviours describes the abuse of alcohol and their remedies. The different phases from the initiation to alcohol dependence which causes various cognitive and physical impairments are explained in details. The abuse of alcohol is here regarded as a behavioural disease which causes considerable private and social costs. Hence, possible prevention and treatment and their effectiveness, together with harm minimization as a viable strategy, are discussed. An analysis of various economic remedies to reduce alcohol abuse, including the effect of elasticities and the effect of minimum price policies on the abuse of alcohol, has also been discussed in details and compared with taxation policies. A discussion on the politics of corporate and social responsibilities will then follow.

Keywords Abuse of alcohol as a behavioural disease · Harmonization of international trade

This book concludes the second volume on the "Economics of Addictive Behaviours". This book describes in details the different phases and pathways from the initiation to alcohol dependence. As the consumption of alcohol becomes chronic, it becomes habitual and the abuser of alcohol eventually becomes dependent and will develop various cognitive and physical impairments.

J. Joshua, *The Economics of Addictive Behaviours Volume II*,
DOI 10.1007/978-3-319-54425-0_10

The consequences of alcohol abuse have been divided into separate sections of physical, psychosocial effects of alcohol abuse and the processes of alcohol abuse and dependence. Alcohol has been described as a psychoactive drug as it contains ethyl alcohol which is a psychoactive ingredient.

This discussion on the consequences of alcohol abuse is followed with a detailed discussion on the prevention and treatment of alcohol abuse. The effectiveness in the intervention and the treatment of alcohol abuse, and the prevention and rehabilitation of alcohol abuse, is followed with a discussion on harm minimization as a viable strategy.

The efficacy of legal remedies to reduce alcohol consumption will depend partly on whether such drugs are legal or illicit. It is argued that effective drug strategies should be an integral policy of harm minimization, for example, the reduction of communicable diseases. To reduce the prevalence of drug use, rehabilitation of drug users, legal remedies to reduce the abuse of alcohol may include educational programmes, conditions of sales, regulations of price promotion and discounts, randomized breath testing and the ban of advertising of alcoholic beverages.

However, educational programmes have not been very successful in reducing alcohol abuse.

It is argued that the harmonization of international trade makes alcoholic beverages cheaper and therefore has detrimental effect on public health. The effects of alcohol abuse on productivity have also been discussed. Chapter 8 includes a detailed discussion on various economic remedies to reduce alcohol abuse, especially in regard to the effect of elasticities on the demand for alcohol and how they affect the outcome of taxation policies. The effect of minimum price policies on the abuse of alcohol has also been discussed in details and compared with taxation policies. The different effects of excise tax when absorbed by producers and when such tax is passed on to consumers have been explained in details. A discussion on the politics of corporate and social responsibilities and corporate responsibilities and social costs will then follow.

The abuse of alcohol is here regarded as a behavioural disease which causes considerable private and social costs. Hence, appropriate policies to curtail the abuse of alcohol have been described.

This second volume of the economics of addictive behaviours describes the abuse of alcohol and the detrimental private and social costs and their remedies. This volume will be followed up with a third volume in the series of addictive behaviour, namely "the abuse of illicit drugs and their remedies" and a fourth volume on the behavioural disease of overeating and its consequences.

References

Aitken, P.P. (1989). Television alcohol commercials and under-age drinking. *International Journal of Advertising*, 8: 133–150.

Aitkin, P.P. and Eadie, D.R. (1988). Television advertisements for alcoholic drinks do reinforce under-age drinking. *British Journal of Addiction*, 83: 1399–1419.

Aitken, P.P. and Eadie, D.R. (1988). Television advertisements for alcoholic drinks do reinforce under-age drinking. *British Journal of Addiction*, 83: 1399–1419.

Ally, A.K., Meng, Y., et al. (2014). Alcohol tax pass-through across the products and price range: do retailers treat cheap alcohol differently. *Addiction*, 109(12): 1994–2002.

American Psychiatric Association. (1994). *Diagnostic and Statistical Manual of Mental Disorders (DSM-IV)* Washington, DC: American Psychiatric Association

American Psychiatric Association. (2013). *Diagnostic and Statistical Manual of Mental Disorders (DSM-5)* Washington, DC: American Psychiatric Association.

Anderson, P. (2012). The impact of alcohol on health; in WHO (2012). In *Alcohol in the European Union: Consumption, harm and policy approaches.* Anderson, P., Møller, L., et al. (Eds.). Copenhagen: WHO Regional Office for Europe.

Anderson, P. and Baumberg, B. (2006). *Alcohol in Europe: A Public Health Perspective.* London: Institute of Alcohol Studies.

Anderson, P., Chisholm, D. and Fuhr, D. (2009). Effectiveness and cost effectiveness of policies and programmes to reduce the harm caused by alcohol. *Lancet*, 373(9682): 2234–2246.

J. Joshua, *The Economics of Addictive Behaviours Volume II*,
DOI 10.1007/978-3-319-54425-0

Arndt, S., Tyrrell, G. et al. (1992). Comorbidity of substance abuse and schizophrenia: The role of pre-morbid adjustment. *Psychological Medicine*, 22: 379–388.

Averett, S.L. and Wang, Y. (2016). Identifying the causal effect of alcohol abuse on the perpetration of intimate partner violence by men using a natural experiment. *Southern Economic Journal*, 82(3): 697–724.

Bandura, A. (1977). *Social Learning Theory*. Englewood Cliffs, NJ: Prentice Hall.

Bandura, A. (1986). *Social foundations of thought and action: A social cognitive theory*. Englewood Cliffs, NJ: Prentice-Hall.

Barbor, T., Caetano, R. et al. (2010). *Alcohol: No Ordinary Commodity. Research and Public Policy*. 2nd ed. Oxford: Oxford University Press.

Barbor, T., et al. (2013). Who is responsible for the public's health? The role of the alcohol industry in the WHO global strategy in harmful use of alcohol. *Addiction*, 108(12): 2045–47.

Becker, G.S., Grossman, M. and Murphy, K.M. (1987). An empirical analysis of cigarette addiction. *Paper presented at the Workshop in the Application of Cigarette Addiction. Presented at the University of Chicago*. May, 18, 1987.

Becker, G.S. (1992). Habits, addictions, and traditions. *Kyklos*, 45(3): 327–45.

Becker, G.S. and Murphy, K.M. (1988). A theory of rational addiction. *Journal of Political Economy*, 96(4): 675–700.

Becker, G.S., Grossman, M. and Murphy, K.M. (1991). Rational addiction and the effect of price on competition. *American Economic Review*, 81(2): 237–241.

Becker, U., Groenbaek, M. et al. (2002). Lower risk for alcohol induced cirrhosis in wine drinkers. *Hepatology*, 35: 868–875.

Bedford, D.A., O'Farrell, A. et al. (2006). Blood alcohol levels in persons who died from accidents and suicide. *Irish Medical Journal*, 99: 80–83.

Bentzen, J. and Smith, V. (2010). Alcohol consumption and liver cirrhoses mortality: New Evidence from a panel data analysis for sixteen European countries. *Working Paper 10–09*. Department of Economics, Aarhus School of Business, University of Aarhus, Aabyhoi, Denmark.

Berkowitz, A.D., and Perkins, H.W. (1987). Current issues in effective alcohol education programming. In *Alcohol Policies and Practices on Colleges and University Campuses*: Vol. 7 National Association of School Psychologists Monograph Series. Sherwood, J.S. (Ed.); pp. 69–85.

Bibb, J.L. and Chambless, D.L. (1986). Alcohol use and abuse among diagnosed agoraphobics. *Behaviour Research and Therapy*, 24: 49–58.

Black, H., Gill, J. et al. (2010). The price of a drink: Levels of consumption and price per unit of alcohol by Edinburgh's ill drinkers with a comparison to wider alcohol sales in Scotland. *Addiction*, 106: 729–736.

Blomgren, J., Martikainen, P. et al. (2004). The effects of regional characteristics on alcohol-related mortality – a register-based multilevel analysis of 1.1 million men. *Social Science & Medicine*, 58: 2523–35.

Bloomfield, K., Gmel, G. et al. (2006). Introduction to special issue 'gender, culture and alcohol problems: A multi-national study'. *Alcohol & Alcoholism*, 41(1): i3–7.

Bobak, M., Room, R. et al. (2004). Contribution of drinking patterns to differences in rates of alcohol related problems between three urban populations. *Journal of Epidemiology & Community Health*, 58(3): 238–242.

Booth, B.M. and Feng, W. (2002). The impact of drinking and drinking consequences on short-term employment outcomes in At_Risk drinkers in six southern states. *Journal of Behavioural Health Services and Research*, 29(2): 157–166.

Booth, B.M., Shields, J.J., and Chandler, R.K. (2009). Recent achievements in alcohol and drug abuse health services research. *Journal of Behavioral Health Services & Research*, 36(1): 5–10.

Borges, G. and Loera, C.R. (2010). Alcohol and drug use in suicidal behaviour. *Current Opinion in Psychiatry*, 23(3): 195–204.

Bourdieu, P. (1984). *Distinction: A Social Critique of the Judgement of Taste.* Translated by R. Nice. London: Routledge & Kegan Paul.

Bozinoff, L., Roth, V. and May, C. (1989). Stages of involvement with drugs and alcohol: Analysis of effects of drug and alcohol abuse advertising. *Advances in Consumer Research*, 16: 215–220.

Brainerd, E. (2001). Economic reform and mortality in the former Soviet Union: A study of the suicide epidemic in 1990s. *European Economic Review*, 45: 1007–1019.

Brown, S.A. and Schuckit, M.A. (1988). Changes in depression among abstinent alcoholics. *Journal of Studies on Alcohol*, 49: 412–417.

Brunn, K. et al. (1975). *Alcohol Control Policies in Public Health Perspective.* Helsinki: Finnish Foundation for Alcohol Studies.

Bureau of Justice Statistics. (1998). *Alcohol and Crime: An Analysis of National Data on the Prevalence of Alcohol Involvement in Crime*, NCJ-168632. Washington, DC: U.S. Department of Justice.

Burki, T. (2010). Changing drinking patterns: A sobering thought. *The Lancet*, 376, 9736: 153–154.

Caces, F.E. and Hartford, T. (1998). Time series analysis of alcohol consumption and suicide mortality in the United States, 1934-1987. *Journal of Studies on Alcohol*, 59: 455–461.

Capuzzi, D. and Lecoq, L.L. (1983). Social and personal determinants of adolescents use and abuse of alcohol and marijuana. *Personnel and Guidance Journal*, 62(4): 199–205.

Carpenter, C. (2005). Heavy alcohol use and the commission of nuisance crime: Evidence from underage drunk driving laws. *The American Economic Review*, 95(2): 267–272.

Carpenter, C. and Dobkin, C. (2009). The effect of alcohol consumption on mortality: Regression discontinuity evidence from minimum drinking age. *American Economic Journal: Applied Economics*, 1(1): 164–82.

Carpenter, C. and Dobkin, C. (2011). The minimum legal drinking age and public health. *Journal of Economic Perspectives*, 25(2): 133–56.

Catalano, R.A., Goldman-Mellor, S. et al. (2011). The health effect of economic decline. Annual *Review of Public Health*, 32: 431–50.

Caulkins, J.P., Pacula, R. et al. (2004). What we can – and cannot – expect from school-based drug prevention. *Drug and Alcohol Review*, 23: 79–87.

Chaloupka, F.J. and Laixuthai, A. (1997). Do youths substitute alcohol and marijuana? Some econometric evidence. *Eastern Economic Journal*, 23(6): 253–276.

Chaloupka, F.J., Saffer, H., and Grossman, M. (1993). Alcohol control policies and motor vehicle fatalities. *Journal of Legal Studies*, 22(1): 161–86.

Chikritzhs, T., Fillmore, K. et al. (2009). A healthy dose of scepticism: Four good reasons to think again about effects of alcohol on coronary heart disease. *Drug Alcohol Review*, 28(4): 441–44.

Chikritzhs, T., Jonas, H. et al. (2001). Mortality and life-years last due to alcohol: A comparison of acute and chronic causes. *Medical Journal of Australia*, 174: 281–284.

Chisholm, D., Doran, C. et al. (2006). Comparative cost-effectiveness of policy instruments for reducing the global burden of alcohol, tobacco and illicit drug use. *Drug and Alcohol Review*, 25: 553–565.

Chisholm, D., Rehm, J. et al. (2004). Reducing the global burden of hazardous alcohol use: A comparative cost-effectiveness analysis. *Journal of the Studies on Alcohol*, 65: 782–93.

Clements, K.W., Lan, Y., and Zhao, X. (2010). The demand for marijuana, tobacco and alcohol: Intercommodity interactions with uncertainty. *Empirical Economics*, 39(1): 203–239.

Cnossen, S. (2007). Alcohol taxation and regulation in the European Union. *International Tax and Public Finance*, 14(6): 699–732. 10.1007/s10797-007-9035-y (accessed 24 November 2008).

Coate, D. and Grossman, M. (1988). Effects of alcoholic beverage prices and legal drinking ages on youth alcohol use. *Journal of Law and Economics*, 31(1):145–71.

Collins, D., Lapsley, H. et al. (2006). *Guidelines for Estimating the Avoidable Costs of Substance Abuse.* Ottawa: Health Canada.

Collins, D.J. and Lapsley, H.M. (1996). *The Social Costs of Drug Abuse in Australia in 1988 and 1992.* Canberra: Australian Government Publishing Services.

Collins, J.J. and Schlenger, W.E. (1988). Acute and chronic effects of alcohol use on violence. *Journal of Studies on Alcohol*, 49: 516–521.

Commonwealth Department of Health and Aged Care. (2001). *Alcohol in Australia: Issues and Strategies: A Background Paper to the National Alcohol Strategy - A Plan for Action 2001 to 2003/04.* Endorsed by the Ministerial Council on Drug Strategy. Canberra: Commonwealth Department of Health and Aged Care.

Cook, P. and Tauchen, G. (1982). The effects of liquor taxes on heavy drinkers. *Bell Journal of Economics*, 13: 255–85.

Cook, P.J., and Moore, M.J. (1993). Taxation of Alcoholic Beverages. In *Economic Research on the Prevention of Alcohol-Related Problems*, Hilton, M. and Bloss, G., Eds. Rockville, MD: NIH Durham No 93–3513.

Cook, P.J. and Moore, M.J. (1994). This tax's for you: The case for higher beer taxes. *National Tax Journal*, 47(3): 559–573.

Cook, P.J. and Moore, M.J. (2002). The economics of alcohol abuse and alcohol-control policies. *Health Affairs*, 21(2): 120–33.

Cook, P.J. and Reuter, P. (2007). When is alcohol just another drug. Some thoughts on research and policy. *Addiction*, 102:1183–1188.

Cook, P.J., Ostermann, J. and Sloan, F.A. (2005, May). The net effect of an alcohol tax increase on death rates in middle age. *The American Economic Review, Papers and Proceedings*, pp. 278–81.

Cooper, S. (1987). The fetal alcohol syndrome. *Journal of Psychology and Psychiatry*, 28: 223–227.

Corrao, G., Rubbiati, L., Bagnardi, V., Zambon, A., and Poikolainen, K. (2000). Alcohol and coronary heart disease: A meta-analysis. *Addiction*, 95(10): 1505–23.

Cotton, N.S. (1979). The familial incidence of alcoholism: A review. *Journal of Studies on Alcohol*, 40(1): 89–116.

De Paulo, P.J, Rubin, M. and Milner, B. (1987). Stages of involvement with alcohol and heroin: Analysis of the effects of marketing on addiction. *Advances in Consumer Research*, 14(1): 521–525

Dee, T.S. (2001). Alcohol abuse and economic conditions: Evidence from repeated cross-sections of individual-level data. *Health Economics*, 10: 257–270.

Degenhardt, L., Lynskey, M. et al. (2000). Cohort trends in the age of initiation of drug use in Australia. *Australian and New Zealand Journal of Public Health*, 24: 421–426.

Department of Health. (2016). *UK Chief Medical Officer's Alcohol Guide*. UK guideline for sensible drinking.

Dollard, J. and Miller, N.E. (1950). *Personality and Psychotherapy*. New York: McGraw-Hill.

Duailibi, S., Ponicki, W. et al. (2007). The effect of restricting opening hours on alcohol-related violence. *American Journal of Public Health*, 97: 2276–280.

Durrance, C.P., Golden, S., Perreira, K. and Cook, P. (2011). Taxing sin and saving lives: Can alcohol taxation reduce female homicides? *Social Science & Medicine*, 73(1): 169–76.

Edwards, G. and Gross, M.M. (1976). Alcohol dependence: Provisional description of a clinical syndrome. *British Medical Journal*, 1: 1058–1061.

Elder, R.W. et al. (2004). Effectiveness of mass media campaigns for reducing drinking and driving and alcohol-involved crashes: A systematic review. *American Journal of Preventive Medicine*, 27: 57–65.

Engberg, J. and Morral, A.R. (2006). Reducing substance use improves adolescents' school attendance. *Addiction*, 101:1741–1751.

Ezzati, M., Hoorn, S.V. et al. (2006). Comparative quantification of mortality and burden of disease attributable to selected risk factors. In *Global Burden of Disease and Risk Factors*. Lopez, A.D. et al. (Eds) New York: Oxford University Press and World Bank.

Ezzati, M., Lopez, A.D., et al. (2004). *Comparative Quantification of Health Risks, Global and Regional Burden of Disease Attributable to Selected Major Risk Factors*. Geneva: World Health Organization.

Faith, M.A., Malcolm, K. and Newgent, R.A. (2009). Reducing potential mental health issues and alcohol abuse through an early prevention model for victims of peer harassment. *Work*, 31(3): 327–335.

Famy, C., Streissguth, A.P., Unis, A.S. (1998). Mental illness in adults with fetal alcohol syndrome or fetal alcohol effects. *American Journal of Psychiatry*, 155(4): 552.

Feinauer, D.M. (1990). The Relationship between workplace accident rates and drug and alcohol and alcohol abuse. The Unproven Hypothesis. *Labor Studies Journal*, Winter(90), 15(4): 3–15.

Fenoglio, P., Parel, V. and Kopp, P. (2003). The social cost of alcohol, tobacco and illicit drugs in France. *European Addiction Research*, 9(1): 18–28.

Finney, J.W. and Monahan, S.C. (1996). The cost-effectiveness of treatment for alcoholism: A second approximation. *Journal of Studies on Alcohol*, 57(3): 229–243.

Fogarty, J.J. (2011). Optimal alcohol taxes for Australia. *Working paper 1120*. School of Agricultural and Resource Economics, University of Western Australia, Crawley, Australia.

Foster, R.K. and Marriott, H.E. (2006). Alcohol consumption in the new millennium – weighting up the risks and benefits for our health. *British Nutrition Foundation Bulletin*, 31:286–331.

Foxcroft, D. (2006a). Alcohol education: Absence of evidence or evidence of absence. *Addiction*, 101: 1057–9.

Foxcroft, D. (2006b). Alcohol misuse prevention for young people: A rapid review of recent evidence. *WHO Technical Report*. School of Health and Social Care, Oxford Brookes University, Oxford.

French, M.T. and Zarkin, G.A. (1995). Is moderate use related to wages? Evidence from four work-sites. *Journal of Health Economics*, 14(3): 319–344.

Gallet, C. (2007). The demand for alcohol: A meta-analysis of elasticities. Australian *Journal of Agricultural Resource Economics*, 51: 121–35.

Garfield, C.F., Chung, P.J. et al. (2003). Alcohol advertising in magazine and adolescents readership. *Journal of American Medical Association*, 289: 2424–2429.

Gavaghan, P.F. (1983). Alcohol industry campaigns against alcohol abuse. *Public Relations Quarterly*, 28(2): 11–16.

Giesbrecht, N. (2007). Reducing alcohol-related damage in populations: Rethinking the roles of education and persuasion interventions. *Addiction*, 102:1345–1349.

Giesbrecht, N., Haydon, E., et al. (2006). Community-based interventions and alcohol, tobacco and other drugs: Foci outcomes and implications. *Drug and Alcohol Review*, 25: 633–646.

Goldstein, B.I., Velyvis, V.P. et al. (2006). The association between moderate alcohol use and illness severity in bipolar disorder. A preliminary report. *Journal of Clinical Psychiatry*, 6791): 102–106.

Goodman, J.K. (1970). Preventing the causes of drug abuse. *Journal of Drug Education*, 2(3) 263–268.

Gorsuch, R.L. and Butler, M.C. (1976). Initial drug abuse: A review of predisposing social psychological factors. *Psychological Bulletin*, 83(1): 120–37.

Graham, D.L. and Gross W.C. (1975). values and attitudes of high school drug users. *Journal of Drug Education*, 5(2): 97–107.

Grossman, M., Sindelar, J.L. Mullahy, J. and Anderson, R. (1993). Alcohol and cigarette taxes. *Journal of Economic Perspectives*, 7(4): 211–22.

Groves, T. (2010). Preventing alcohol related harm to health: Clamp down on alcohol promotion and set a minimum price. *British Medical Journal*, 340 (January): c 372.

Grube, G.W. (1993). Alcohol portrayals and alcohol advertising on television. *Alcohol, Health and Research World*, 17: 6166.

Gutjahr, E., Gmel, G. et al. (2001). Relation between average alcohol consumption and disease: An overview. *European Addiction Research*, 7(3): 117–127.

Heien, D.M. and Pittman, D.J. (1993). The external costs of alcohol abuse. *Journal of Studies on Alcohol*, 54: 302–307.

Helliwell, J.F. (2004). Well-being and social capital: Does suicide pose a puzzle? NBER Working Paper Series. *Working Paper 10896*. National Bureau of Economic Research, Cambridge, MA.

Hingson, R. and Winter, M. (2003). Epidemiology and consequences of drinking and driving. *Alcohol Research and Health*, 27(1): 63–78.

Hufford, M.R. (2001). Alcohol and suicidal behaviour. *Clinical Psychological Review*, 21: 797–811.

Irving, H.M., Samokhvalov, A.V., et al. (2009). Alcohol as a risk factor for pancreatitis. A systematic review and meta-analysis. *Journal of the Pancreas*, 10(4): 387–92.

Jellinek, E.M. (1952). Phases of alcohol addiction. *Quarterly Journal of Studies on Alcohol*, 13: 673–683.

Johansson, E., Alho, H. et al. (2007). The association of alcohol dependency with employment probability: Evidence from the population survey 'Health 2000 in Finland'. *Health Economics*, 16: 739–54.

Jones, S.C., Hall, D. et al. (2008). How effective is the revised regulatory code for alcohol advertising in Australia? *Drug Alcohol Review*, 27(1): 29–38.

Kenkel, D.S. (1993). Drinking, driving, and deterrence: The social costs of alternative policies. *Journal of Law and Economics*, 36(2): 877–913.

Kenkel, D.S. (1996, April). New estimates of the optimal tax on alcohol. *Economic Inquiry*, 34(2): 296–319.

Kenkel, D.S. (2005). Are alcohol tax hikes fully passed through to prices? Evidence from Alaska. *The American Economic Review*, 95(2): 273–277.

Kerr, W.C., Fillmore, K.M. et al. (2000). Beverage- specific alcohol consumption and cirrhoses mortality in a group of English-speaking beer-drinking countries. *Addiction*, 95: 339–346.

Kia-Keating, M., Brown, S.A., Schulte, M.T. and Monreal, T. K (2009, July). Adolescent satisfaction with brief motivational enhancement for alcohol abuse. The *Journal of Behavioral Health Services & Research*, 36(3): 385–395.

Klatsky, A.L., Armstrong, M.A. et al. (1990). Correlates of alcoholic beverage preference: Traits of persons who choose wine, liquor or beer. *Addiction*, 85(10): 1279–89.

Kotler, P. and Roberto, E.L. (1989). *Social Marketing: Strategies for Changing Public Behaviour*. New York: The Free Press.

Lehto, J. (1997). The economics of alcohol. *Addiction*, 92(Supplement 1): S55–S59

Laranjeira, R. and Mitsuhiro, S.S. (2010). Addiction research centres and the nurturing of creativity. National institute on alcohol and drugs policies, Brazil. *Addiction*, 107: 727–732.

Lester, D. (1998). Suicide and homicide after the fall of communist regimes. *European Psychiatry*, 13: 98–100.

Lettierie, D.J., Mollie, S., et al. (1980). Theories on Drug Abuse: Selected Contemporary Perspectives (*NIDA Research Monograph N. 30)*. Rockville, MD: National Institute on Drug Abuse.

Livingston, M. (2010). A longitudinal analysis of alcohol outlet density and domestic violence. *Addiction*, 106(5): 919–25.

MacDonald, Z. and Shields, M. (2004). Does problem drinking affect employment? Evidence from England. *Health Economics*, 13: 139–55.

Mäkelä, P. (1999a). Alcohol-related mortality as a function of socio-economic status. *Addiction*, 94: 867–86.

Mäkelä, P. (1999b). Alcohol related mortality during an economic boom and recession. *Contemporary Drug Problems*, 26: 369–390.

Manafò, E. and Giesbrecht, N. (2011). Alcohol, cancer and other health issues: An action plan for prevention. *A Report to the Toronto Cancer Prevention Coalition*. Toronto.

Markowitz, S. (2000). The price of alcohol, wife abuse and husband abuse. *Southern Economic Journal*, 67(2): 279–303.

Markowitz, S., Kaestner, R. and Grossman, M. (2005, May). An investigation of the effects of alcohol consumption and alcohol policies on youth risky sexual behaviors. *The American Economic Review*, 95(2): 263–266.

Martin, J., Barry, J. et al. (2010). Alcohol-attributable mortality in Ireland. *Alcohol and Addiction*, 45: 379–386.

Mattson, S.N., Riley, E.P., Grambling, L. et al. (1998). Neuropsychological comparison of alcohol – exposed children with or without physical. *Neuropsychology*, 12; 146–153.

Maynard, A. and O'Brien, B. (1982). Harmonisation policies in the European community and alcohol abuse. *British Journal of Addiction*, 77: 235–44.

Mazzaglia, G., Britton, A.R. (2001). Exploring the relationship between alcohol consumption and non-fatal or fatal stroke: Systematic review. *Addiction*, 96: 1743–1756.

McBride, N., Farringdon, F. et al. (2004). Harm minimization in school drug education: Final results of the School Health and Alcohol Harm Reduction Project (SHAHRP). *Addiction*, 99: 278–291.

McGregor, D., Murray, R.P. et al. (2003). Personality differences between users of wine, beer and spirits in a community sample: The Winnipeg health and drinking survey. *Journal of Studies on Alcohol*, 64: 634–41.

Meier, P.S., Purshouse, R. and Brennan, A. (2009). Policy options for alcohol price regulation: The importance of modelling population heterogeneity. *Addiction*, 105: 383–393.

Miller, S.M. and Moulton, S. (2014). Publicness in policy environment. A multi-level analysis of substance abuse treatment services. *Journal of Public Administration & Research Theory*, 24(3): 553–589.

Mills, T.C. (2007). Liver cirrhosis and alcohol consumption in the U.K.: Series modelling of recent trends. *Statistical Modelling*, 7: 91–103.

Miron, J.A. and Zwiebel, J. (1991). Alcohol consumption during prohibition. *American Economic Review*, 81(2): 242–247.

Miron, J.A. and Zwiebel, J. (1995). The economic case against drug prohibition. *Journal of Economic Perspectives*, 9(4): 175–192.

Moskowitz, H. and Fiorentino, D. (2000). *A Review of the Literature on the Effects of Low Doses of Alcohol on Driving Related Skills*. Springfield, VA: US Department of Transportation, National Highway Traffic Safety Administration.

Moskowitz, S. (1989). The primary prevention of alcohol problems: A critical review of the research literature. *Journal of Studies on Alcohol*, 50(1): 54–88

Mullahy, J. and Sindelar, J.L. (1990). An ounce of prevention: Productive Remedies for Alcoholism. *Journal of Policy Analysis and Management*, 9(2): 249–53.

Mullahy, J. and Sindelar, J.L. (1991). Gender differences on labor market effects of alcoholism. *American Economic Review*, 81(2): 161–165.

Mullahy, J. and Sindelar, J.L. (1993). Alcoholism, work and income. *Journal of Labor Economics*, 11(3): 494–520).

Mullahy, J. and Sindelar, J.L. (1994a). Alcoholism and income: The role of indirect effects. *Milbank Quarterly*, 72(2): 359–75.

Mullahy, J. and Sindelar, J.L. (1994b). Alcoholism, work, and income over the life cycle. *Working Papers*, 11(3); pp. 494–520. National Bureau of Economic Research, Cambridge, MA.

Mullahy, J. and Sindelar, J.L. (1996). Employment, unemployment, and problem drinking. *Journal of Health Economics*, 15: 409–34.

Nelson, D.E., Jarman, D.W. et al. (2013). Alcohol-attributable cancer deaths and years of potential life lost in the United States. *American Journal of Public Health*, 103(4): 641–8.

Norström, T. (1995). Alcohol and suicide: A comparative analysis of France and Sweden. *Addiction*, 90: 1463–1469.

Nutt, D., King, L.A. et al. (2007). Development of a rational scale to access the harm of drugs of potential misuse. *The Lancet*, 369: 1047–53.

Nutt, D.J., King, L.A. et al. (2010). Drug harms in the U.K.: A multicriteria decision analysis. *Lancet*, 376(9752): 1558–65.

O'Brien, A, Leonard, L. et al. (2012). Could an advance practice nurse improve detection of alcohol misuse in the emergency department? *International Journal of Mental Health Nursing*, 21: 340–348.

Ogwang, T. and Cho, D.I. (2009). Economic determinants of the consumption of alcoholic beverages in Canada: A panel data analysis. *Empirical Economics*, 37(3): 599–613.

Olshansky, S., Passaro, D.J. et al. (2005). A potential decline in life expectancy in the United States in the 21st century. *New England Journal of Medicine*, 352(11): 1138–1145.

Orford, J., Hodgson, R. et al. (2006). The clients' perspective on change during treatment for an alcohol problem: Qualitative analysis of follow-up interviews in the UK Alcohol Treatment Trial. *Addiction*, 101(1): 60–68.

Pacula, R.L. (1998). Does increasing the beer tax reduce marijuana consumption? *Journal of Health Economics*, 17(5): 57–85.

Pan, S., Fang, C. et al. (2006). Alcoholic beverage consumption in China: A censored demand system approach. *Applied Economics Letters*, 13(15): 975–79.

Parry, C., Myers, B. et al. (2003). The case for an increased tax on alcohol in South Africa. *South African Journal of Economics*, 71(2): 137–145.

Parry, C.D.H. and Dewing, S. (2006). A public health approach to addressing alcohol- related crime in South Africa. *African Journal of Drug and Alcohol Studies*, 5(1): 41–56.

Parry, I.W.H. and West, S.E. (2004). Fiscal and externality arguments for alcohol taxes. *97th Annual Conference on Taxation. National Tax Association Proceedings*; pp. 12–18. Minniapolis.

Parry, I.W.H., Laxminarayan, R. et al. (2006). Fiscal and externality rationales for alcohol taxes, revised 2009. *Discussion Paper*. Resources for the Future, Washington, DC.

Patra, J. et al. (2010). Alcohol consumption and the risk of morbidity and mortality from different stroke types – a systematic review and meta-analysis. *BMC Public Health*, 10: 258.

Penberthy, J.K., Ait-Daoud, N., et al. (2007). Evaluating readiness and treatment seeking effects in a pharmacotherapy trial for alcohol dependence. *Alcoholism: Clinical and Experimental Research*, 31(9): 1538–1544.

Perkins, H.W. and Berkowitz, A.D. (1991). Collegiate COAs and alcohol abuse: Problem drinking in relation to assessment of parents and grandparents alcoholism. *Journal of Counseling & Development*, 69(3): 237–240.

Peterson, J.B., Rothfleisch, J. et al. (1990). Acute alcohol intoxication and neuropsychological functioning. *Journal of Studies on Alcohol*, 51: 114–122.

Phelps, C.E. (1988). Death and taxes: An opportunity for substitution. *Journal of Health Economics*, 7(7): 1–24.

Pogue, T.F. and Sgontz, L.G. (1989). Taxing to control social costs: The case of alcohol. *American Economic Review*, 79(1): 235–243.

Popova, S., Patra, J. et al. (2012). Cost of privatisation versus government alcohol retailing systems: Canadian example. *Drug and Alcohol Review*, 31: 4–12.

Popovici, I. and French, M.T. (2013). Does unemployment lead to greater alcohol consumption? *Industrial Relations*, 52(2): 444–466.

Puffer, R. and Griffith, G.W. (1967). *Patterns of Urban Mortality*. Washington, DC: Pan American Health Organization.

Rabinovich, L., Brutscher, P. et al. (2009). *The Affordability of Alcoholic Beverages in the European Union. Understanding the Link between Alcohol Affordability, Consumption and Harms*. Cambridge: RAND Europe.

Ramful, P. and Zhao, X., (2008). Individual heterogeneity in alcohol consumption: The case of beer, wine and spirits in Australia. *The Economic Record*, 265: 207–22.

Ramstedt, M. (2001a). Per capita alcohol consumption and liver cirrhosis mortality in 14 European countries. *Addiction*, 96: 19–34.

Ramstedt, M. (2001b). Alcohol and suicide in 14 European countries. *Addiction*, 96: 59–75.

Ramstedt, M. (2002). Alcohol-related mortality in 15 European countries in post-war period. In *Alcohol in Postwar Europe, Consumption, Drinking Patterns,*

Consequences and Policy Responses in 15 European Countries. Norström, T. (Ed.) Stockholm: Almqvist and Wiksell International; pp.137–156.

Ramstedt, M. (2003). Alcohol consumption and liver cirrhosis mortality with and without mention of alcohol – the case of Canada. *Addiction*, 98(9): 1267–1276.

Rayner, T. and Chetwynd, J. (1987). The economic costs of alcohol-related health care in New Zealand. *British Journal of Addiction*, 82(82): 59–66.

Razvodovsky, Y.E. (2011). Alcohol consumption and suicide in Belarus, 1980-2005. *Suicidology Online*, 2011(2): 1–7.

Rehm, J. (2011). The risks associated with alcohol use and alcoholism. *Alcohol Research & Health*, 34(2): 135–143.

Rehm, J. and Shield, K.D. (2013). Alcohol and mortality: Global alcohol-attributable deaths from cancer, liver cirrhosis and injury in 2010. *Alcohol Research: Current Reviews*, 35(2): 174–183.

Rehm, J. et al. (2010a). The relation between different dimensions of alcohol consumption and burden of disease – an overview. *Addiction*, 105: 817–843.

Rehm, J. et al. (2010b). Alcohol as a risk factor for liver cirrhosis: A systematic review and meta-analysis. *Drug Alcohol Review*, 29: 437–45.

Rehm, J., Gmel, G.; Sempos, C. and Trevisan, M. (2003). Alcohol-related morbidity and morbidity and mortality. *Alcohol Research and Health*, 27(1): 39–51.

Rehm, J., Gutjahr, E. and Gmel, G. (2001). Alcohol and all-cause mortality: A pooled analysis. *Contemporary Drug Problems*, 28(3): 337–62.

Rehm, J., Mathers, C. et al. (2009). Global burden of disease and injury and economic cost attributable to alcohol use and alcohol-use disorders. *Lancet*, 373: 2223–33.

Renna, F. (2008). Alcohol abuse, alcoholism, and labor market outcomes: Looking for the missing link. *Industrial and Labor Relations Review*, 62(1): 92–103.

Reynolds, K., Lewis, L.B. et al. (2003). Alcohol consumption and risk of stroke. *Journal of the American Medical Association*, 289(5): 579–588.

Richardson, J. and Crowley, S. (1994). Optimum alcohol taxation: Balancing consumption and external costs. *Health Economics*, 3(2): 73–87.

Rimm, E.E., Giovannucci, E.L., et al. (1991, August 24). Prospective study of alcohol consumption and risk of coronary disease in men. *The Lancet*, 338: 464–68.

Ritter, A. and Cameron, J. (2006). A review of the efficacy and effectiveness of harm reduction strategies for alcohol, tobacco and illicit drugs. *Drugs and Alcohol Review*, 25: 611–624.

Roizen, J. (1993). Issues in the epidemiology of alcohol and violence. In *Alcohol and Interpersonal Violence: Fostering Interdisciplinary Violence Perspectives* Martin, S.E. Ed. Rockville, MD: National Institute of Health.

Room, R., Barbor, T. et al. (2005). Alcohol and public health. *Lancet*, 365: 519–529.

Rosenhan, D.L. and Seligman, M.E.P. (1984). *Abnormal Psychology.* New York and London, W.W. Norton and Co.

Rossow, I. (1996). Alcohol and suicide – beyond the link at the individual level. *Addiction*, 91: 1463–1469.

Sacco, R.L., Elkind, M. et al. (1999). The protection effect of moderate alcohol consumption in ischemic stroke. *Journal of the American Medical Association*, 281(1): 53–60.

Saffer, H. and Grossman, M. (1987a, July). Drinking age laws and highways mortality rates: Cause and effect. *Economic Inquiry*, 24: 403–18.

Saffer, H. and Grossman, M. (1987b). Beer taxes, the legal drinking age, and youth motor vehicle fatalities. *Journal of Legal Studies*, 16(2): 351–74.

Samokhvalov, A.V., Irving, H.M. et al. (2010). Alcohol as a risk factor for atrial fibrillation: A systematic review and meta-analysis. *European Journal of Cardiovascular Prevention and Rehabilitation*, 17: 706–712.

Sarafino, E.P. (1990). *Health Psychology: Biopsychosocial Interactions*. New York: John Wiley & Sons.

Savell, E., Fooks, G. et al. (2016). How does the alcohol industry attempt to influence marketing regulations? A systematic review. *Addiction*, 111(1): 18–32.

Sayette, M.A., Wilson, T. et al. (1993). Alcohol and Aggression: A social information processing analysis. *Journal of Studies on Alcohol*, 54: 399–407.

Schaeffer, E. and Ritz, E. (2012). Alcohol and Kidney damage: A Janus-faced relationship. *Kidney International*, 81(9): 816–8.

Schneider, M., Norman, R. et al. (2007). Estimating the burden of disease attributable to alcohol use in South Africa in 2000. *South African Medical Journal*, 97: 664–672.

Shahandeh, B. (1985). Drug and alcohol abuse in the workplace: Consequences and counter measures. *International Labour Review*, 124(2): 207–221.

Shield, K.D., Parry, C. et al. (2013). Chronic diseases and conditions related to alcohol use. *Alcohol Research Current Reviews*, 35: 155–171.

Single, E. (2009). Why we should still estimate the costs of substance abuse even if we needn't pay undue attention to the bottom line. *Drug and Alcohol Review*, 282: 117–121.

Single, E., Robson, L. and Xie, X. (1996). *The Costs of Substance Abuse in Canada: A Cost Estimation Study: Full Report*. Ottawa: Canadian Centre on Substance Abuse (CCSA).

Smith, S.W., Atkin, C.K. et al. (2006). Are "Drink Responsibility" alcohol campaigns strategically ambiguous? *Health Communication*, 20(1): 1–11.

Stockwell, T., Auld, M.C. et al (2011). Does minimum pricing reduce alcohol consumption? The experience of a Canadian province. *Addiction*, 107(5): 912–920.

Stranges, S., Wu, T. et al. (2004). Relationship of alcohol drinking pattern to risk of hypertension: A population-based study. *Hypertension*, 44: 813–19.

Stuckler, D. et al. (2009). The public health effect of economic crises and alternative policy responses in Europe: An empirical analysis. *Lancet*, 374: 315–323.

Sturgess, J.E., George, T.P. et al. (2011). Pharmacogenetics of alcohol, nicotine and drug addiction treatments. *Addiction Biology*, 16: 357–376.

Substance Abuse and Mental Health Services. (2013). *Substance abuse: statistics and quality*. Rockville, MD: Center for Behavioral Health Statistics and Quality (SAMHS).

Taylor, B. et al. (2009). Alcohol and hypertension: Gender differences in dose-response relationships determined through systematic review and meta- analysis. *Addiction*, 104: 1981–1990.

Teesson, M., Newton, N. et al. (2012). Australian school-based prevention programs for alcohol and other drugs: A systematic review. *Drug and Alcohol Review*, 31: 731–736.

Terza, J.V. (2002). Alcohol abuse and employment: A second look. *Journal of Applied Econometrics*, 17: 393–404.

The Home Office. (2012). *Drugs and Alcohol Unit: The Governments Alcohol Strategy*. London: The Home Office.

The New Zealand Medical Association (NZMA). (2015). Reducing alcohol-related harm – Policy Briefing. www.nzma.org.nz.

Thompson, A., Bradley, E. et al. (1997). A Qualitative investigation of the responses of in-treatment and recovering heavy drinkers to alcohol advertising on New Zealand television. *Contemporary Drug Problems*, 24(1): 133–146.

van Gils, P.F., Hamberg-van Reenen, H. et al. (2010). The scope of costs in alcohol studies: Cost-of-illness studies differ from economic evaluation. *Cost Effectiveness Resource Allocation*, 8: 15. Bio Med Central. http://www.resource-allocation.com/content/8/1/15.

van Iwaarden, M.J. (1989). An economist in 'alcohol policy country'. *British Journal of Addiction*, 84: 1205–1216.

Volpicelli, J.R. (2001). Alcohol abuse and alcoholism: An overview. *Journal of Clinical Psychiatry*, 62: 4–10.

von Hinke Kessler Scholder, S., Wehby, G.L., Lewis, S. and Zuccolo, L. (2014, May). Alcohol exposure in utero and child academic achievement. *The Economic Journal*, 124: 634–667.

Wagenaar, A.C., Salois, M.J. and Komro, K.A. (2009). Effects of beverage alcohol price and tax levels on drinking: A meta-analysis of 1003 estimates from 112 studies. *Addiction*, 104:179–190.

Wagstaff, A. (1987). Government prevention policy and the relevance of social cost estimates. *British Journal of Addiction*, 82: 461–467.

Wallack, L., Grube, J.W. et al. (1990). Portrayals of alcohol on prime-time television. *Journal of Studies on Alcohol*, 51: 428–37.

Walsh, B. and Walsh, D. (2011). Suicide in Ireland: The influence of alcohol and unemployment. *The Economic and Social Review*, 42(1): 27–47.

Wiggins, J.A. and Wiggens, B.B. (1987). Drinking at a Southern University: Its description and correlate. *Journal of Studies on Alcohol*, 48(4): 319–324.

Wiist, W.H. (2010). *The Bottom Line or Public Health: Tactics Corporations Use to Influence Health and Health Policy, and What We Can Do to Counter Them.* Oxford: Oxford University Press.

Wiley, J.A. and Weisner, C. (1995). Drinking in violent and nonviolent events leading to arrest: Evidence from a survey of arrestees. *Journal of Criminal Justice*, 23: 461–476.

Willenbring, M.L. (1986). Measurement of depression in alcoholics. *Journal of Studies on Alcohol*, 49: 412–417.

Willenbring, M.L. (2014). Gaps in clinical prevention and treatment for alcohol use disorders – cost, consequences, and strategies. *Alcohol Research Current Reviews*, 35(2): 238–43.

Wills, T.A. (1986). Stress and coping in early adolescence: Relationships to substance use in urban school samples. *Health Psychology*, 5: 503–529.

Wodak, A. and Cooney, A. (2005). Effectiveness of sterile needle and syringe programmes. *International Journal of Drug Policy*, 16: 31–44.

World Health Organization. (1980). Problems related to alcohol consumption. *Report of a WHO Expert Committee.* Technical Report Series No. 650. Geneva: World Health Organization.

World Health Organization. (2004a). *WHO-CHOICE Cost-Effectiveness Analysis.* Geneva: World Health Organization. http://www.who.int/who.sis

World Health Organization. (2004b). *Global Status Report on Alcohol.* Geneva: World Health Organization.

World Health Organization. (2004c). *Effectiveness of Sterile Needle and Syringe Programming in Reducing HIV/AIDS Among Injecting Drug Users.* Geneva: World Health Organization.

World Health Organization. (2004d). *Neuroscience of Psychoactive Substance Use and Dependence.* Geneva: World Health Organization.

World Health Organization. (2005). *World Health Multi-County on Women's Health and Domestic Violence Against Women: Initial Results on Prevalence, Health Outcomes and Women's Responses.* Geneva: World Health Organization.

World Health Organization. (2007). *International Classification of Diseases (ICD) and Related Health Problems*; 10th Revision. Geneva: World Health Organization.

World Health Organization. (2009). *Evidence for the Effectiveness and Cost-Effectiveness of Interventions to Reduce Alcohol-Related Harm.* Copenhagen: World Health Organization Regional Office for Europe.

World Health Organization. (2011). *Global Status Report on Alcohol and Health.* Geneva: World Health Organization.

World Health Organization. (2012). *Alcohol in the European Union: Consumption, harm and policy approaches.* Anderson, P., Møller, L. et al. (eds). Copenhagen: WHO Regional Office for Europe.

World Health Organization. (2014). *Global Status Report on Alcohol and Health*. Geneva: World Health Organization.

Xu, X. and Chaloupka, F.J. (2011). The effects of prices on alcohol use and its consequences. *Alcohol Research & Health*, 34(2): 236–245.

Zachry, W.M., Grizzle, A.J., et al. (2002). Understanding the costs and treatment of alcohol abuse and dependence. *Practical Pharmacoeconomics*, 37(8): 407–416.

Zarkin, G.A., French, M.P. et al. (1998). Alcohol use and wages: New results from the National Household Survey on Drug Abuse. *Journal of Health Economics*, 17(1): 53–68.

Index

A

Alcohol
- abuse *vs.* misuse, 1, 2, 3, 4, 7, 8, 9, 11, 12, 13, 16, 17, 18, 21, 23, 24, 25, 26, 27, 28, 31, 32, 33, 34, 37, 38, 39, 40, 41, 42, 43, 44, 47, 48, 50, 51, 52, 53, 60, 62, 63, 64, 65, 66, 67, 68, 69, 70, 73, 77, 78, 79, 80, 81, 82, 83, 85, 86, 88, 89, 90, 91, 92, 94, 95, 98, 99, 101, 102
- anxiolytic use of alcohol, 19, 32
- conditions of sales, 3, 49, 52, 102
- dependence, 1, 2, 3, 9, 11–18, 19, 20, 22, 29, 30, 31, 32, 38, 40, 43, 57, 64, 98, 101, 102
- dependence - Diagnostic and Statistical Manual IV – (DSM – IV), 28, 30
- drink-driving, 39, 47, 49, 50, 52, 54, 55, 57, 65
- educational impact, 3, 49, 50, 52
- effect, physiological, 3, 4, 20, 24, 30, 32, 68; psychological-social, 3, 19, 24, 102
- immunosuppressant, 17, 20
- industry; self-regulation, 4, 93, 94, 96, 97
- marijuana and alcohol; legalization, 35, 46; decriminalization, 34, 35
- marketing strategy, 4, 52, 56, 95
- price promotion, discounts, 3, 49, 53, 102
- processes of alcohol abuse and dependence, 3, 19, 29, 102
- prohibition, 19, 34, 46
- psychoactive, psychotropic drug, 1, 2, 5, 6, 7, 19, 24, 31, 47, 50, 102
- reasons for drinking alcohol, 33
- toxic substance, 18
- use, legal remedies, 1, 3, 49–57, 102

Alcohol abuse
- absenteeism, 38, 64, 67, 68
- adolescents, 8, 16, 18, 20, 25, 26, 30, 33, 34, 56, 80, 94, 96
- aggressive behaviour, 28, 29
- alcoholism, 21, 30, 32, 41, 44, 66, 67, 68, 86, 87, 89
- anxiety, 13, 21, 26, 31
- causes, 1, 2, 9, 11–18, 20, 22, 27, 32, 33, 38, 45, 46, 47, 65, 69, 101, 102
- consequences; physiological effects, 3, 19; psycho-social effects, 3, 19, 24, 102

J. Joshua, *The Economics of Addictive Behaviours Volume II*,
DOI 10.1007/978-3-319-54425-0

Alcohol abuse (*cont.*)
depression, 21, 22, 26, 27, 32, 43, 66
detrimental effects, 2, 3, 7, 14, 16, 17, 18, 20, 23, 38, 39, 40, 41, 43, 50, 51, 52, 54, 55, 59, 61, 63, 64, 65, 68, 70, 78, 85, 91, 94, 98
Diagnostic and Statistical Manual (DSM 5), 30, 38
diseases, acute, 1, 2, 11, 15, 18, 29; chronic, 1, 2, 9, 11, 14, 15, 16, 17, 18, 20, 21, 23, 28, 29, 30, 32, 77, 98, 101
drink-driving, 39, 47, 49, 50, 52, 54, 55, 57, 65
drugs, prevention programs, 33, 45, 50, 51
economic remedies, 1, 4, 60, 73–92, 101, 102
education, 3, 16, 26, 31, 39, 40, 43, 49, 50, 51, 52, 56, 57, 66, 94, 102
employment, unemployment, 2, 3, 11, 12, 13, 14, 26, 27, 35, 45, 60, 64, 66, 68, 85, 97, 98
evaluation, 33, 43, 45, 47, 65
government intervention, 3, 37, 52
gynaecological patients, 60, 66
initiation, 1, 2, 11–18, 29, 41, 88, 94, 96, 101
living conditions, 2, 11, 12
loss in productivity, 60, 64, 67, 69, 71
mortality, 6, 9, 10, 13, 22, 23, 27, 32, 42, 47, 56, 63, 88, 90
pathways from initiation to alcohol dependence, 2, 14
pharmacogenetics, 3, 43, 44
phases, from initiation to alcohol dependence, 1, 2, 11, 14
policy mix, 41, 74
presenteeism, 38, 64
prevention, 1, 2, 3, 11, 14, 25, 33, 37–48, 50, 51, 62, 69, 70, 80, 101, 102
processes, 3, 16, 18, 19, 20, 31, 41, 42, 62, 102
rehabilitation, 3, 37, 38, 45, 48, 55, 65, 102
remedies, 1, 2, 3, 4, 47, 49–57, 60, 73–92, 101, 102
risk factors, 1, 2, 5, 9, 11, 12
self-medication, 3, 19, 29, 31, 32
social and private costs, 3, 4, 38, 59–71
social problems, acute, 2, 9
social problems, chronic, 15, 29
socio-demographics, 2, 12
stress, 12, 13, 17, 26, 29, 30, 41, 44, 68
suicide, 2, 3, 9, 11, 13, 14, 21, 26, 27, 28
taxation, 1, 4, 34, 38, 44, 49, 50, 57, 62, 63, 73, 76, 78, 80, 81, 83, 84, 97, 101, 102
treatment, 1, 2, 3, 11, 14, 15, 16, 30, 32, 37–48, 54, 55, 57, 64, 65, 66, 84, 101, 102
violence, 9, 10, 16, 18, 22, 24, 25, 27, 28, 33, 34, 38, 46, 47, 52, 53, 63, 85
violence, intimate partner violence, 24, 25
world-wide risk, 1, 2, 5, 9
Alcohol consumption
-Australia, 8, 9, 22, 25, 48, 51, 55, 56, 67, 87
- Beer, 8, 19, 22, 23, 33, 53, 67, 77, 78, 79, 80, 81, 82, 83, 85, 87, 96
communicable diseases, 17, 18, 20, 48, 102
consequences, HIV/AIDS, 18, 22, 48

dependence; processes, 3, 16, 18, 19, 29, 31, 41, 42, 62, 102
England, 7, 81
European community, 7
foetal alcohol syndrome, 21, 22, 60, 65, 66
Germany, 8
hazardous drinkers, 33, 54, 81, 82
liver cirrhosis, 20, 22, 23, 39, 63
non-communicable diseases, 17
non-hazardous drinkers, 33
operant conditioning, 16
patterns of alcohol consumption, 1, 2, 5, 6, 11, 17; volume, 5, 6, 7, 17, 23, 96; frequency, 17, 18, 80; outlets, 28, 39, 40, 49, 50, 52, 53, 57, 61, 77, 84
pregnancy, 3, 21, 52
prenatal alcohol exposure, 21
Russia, 7
spirits, 8, 19, 22, 23, 53, 77, 78, 80, 81
wine, 8, 19, 22, 23, 33, 40, 53, 77, 78, 80, 82, 83, 86, 87, 96
world-wide, 13

Alcoholism, *see* Alcohol abuse, alcoholism
Alcohol use, lifestyle
anxiolytic use, 19, 32
legal remedies, 3, 49–57, 102
self-medication, 3, 19, 29, 31, 32
American Psychiatric Association, 3, 29, 30
Anderson, P., 17, 18, 20, 22, 27, 43, 50, 54, 56, 57, 64, 65, 77, 78, 80, 83, 87
Anxiety, *see* Alcohol abuse, anxiety

B

Bandura, A., 16, 26
Barbor, T., 7, 99
Baumberg, B., 18, 22, 27, 43, 50, 54, 64, 65, 77, 83, 87
Becker, G. S., 34, 60, 80, 90
Becker, U., 23
Behavioural diseases, 1, 2, 9, 38, 41, 51, 62, 63, 87, 97, 101, 102
Behavioural modification, 3, 49, 50
Binge drinking, 5, 6, 7, 40, 61, 81
Blood alcohol content (BAC), 28, 39, 54

C

Cancer, cavity, pharynx, liver, colon, rectum, breast, lung cancer, 9, 10, 16, 17, 18, 20, 23
Car accidents, 3, 9, 20, 28, 42, 49, 50, 60, 64, 80
Cardiovascular diseases, 9, 10, 17, 18, 32
Causes of alcohol abuse, *see* Alcohol abuse, causes
Chronic diseases, cancer, 9, 11, 15, 16, 18, 20, 29, 30, 32
Consequences of alcohol abuse, *see* Alcohol abuse, consequences
Consumption of alcohol
consumption, beer, spirits, wine, 8, 22, 23, 33, 53, 78, 79, 82, 84, 87
consumption pattern, 2, 5, 6, 7, 11, 17, 18, 22, 29, 30, 74, 94
patterns of the consumption of alcohol, (*see* Alcohol consumption, patterns of alcohol consumption)
Cook, P. J., 42, 63, 79, 88, 89
Corporate and social responsibilities
marketing strategy, 4, 52, 56, 95
politics, 4, 7, 93–99, 101, 102
self-regulation, 4, 93, 94, 96, 97

D

Dependence, *see* Alcohol, dependence
Depression, *see* Alcohol abuse, depression
Diagnostic Statistical Manual (DSM-IV; DSM-5), 29
Disability, adjusted life years (DALYs), 9
Diseases, acute
  chronic, (*see* Alcohol abuse, diseases chronic)
  See also Alcohol abuse, diseases acute
Dollard, J., 41
Drink-driving, *see* Alcohol abuse, drink-driving
Drinking, binge, 5, 6, 7, 17, 40, 61, 81
Drugs, illicit, 1, 4, 15, 16, 24, 29, 31, 39, 42, 46, 47, 48, 50, 51, 53, 67, 84, 102
Drugs, prevention programmes, *see* Alcohol abuse, drug prevention programmes

E

Educational impact on the abuse of alcohol, 3, 49, 50, 52
Effects, detrimental, *see* Alcohol abuse, detrimental effects
Effects, social and private costs, *see* Alcohol abuse, social and private costs
Effects, psycho-social, *see* Alcohol abuse, psycho-social effects
Elasticities
  cross-elasticities, 42, 77
  cross-price, 34, 42, 73, 74, 75, 77, 79, 82, 83, 92
  demand for alcohol, 4, 40, 56, 74, 83, 84, 89, 96, 98, 102
  price, sensitive, 77
  taxation policies; substitution effect, 79, 92; inelastic, elastic, 4, 34, 35, 42, 46, 60, 73, 74, 75, 76, 77, 79, 81, 82, 83, 88, 92, 102
Employment, 12, 13, 14, 35, 45, 66, 68, 85, 97, 98
Ethanol, 6, 21, 43, 54
Ethyl alcohol, 5, 6, 24, 102
  metabolism, 43
Excise tax, absorbed by producers, 73
  passed on to consumers, 73, 78, 80, 102

F

Foetal alcohol syndrome, *see* Alcohol consumption, foetal alcohol syndrome

G

Gastrointestinal conditions, 18
Giesbrecht, N., 10, 43, 50, 52
Grossman, M., 78, 79, 80, 88, 90

H

Harm minimization, 3, 38, 39, 47, 48, 50, 101, 102
HIV/AIDS, 18, 22, 48

I

International Classification of diseases, revision 10 (ICD-10), 20
International trade agreement, 4, 62, 63
  effects on health, 2, 5, 52, 63, 83

J
Jellinek, E. M., 14

K
Kenkel, D. S., 56, 60, 78, 80, 81
Korsakoff-Wernicke syndrome, 3, 21

L
Legal remedies, *see* Alcohol use, legal remedies
Liver cirrhoses, 9, 18, 22, 23

M
Marketing, social, 26, 95
Market, social and private costs, 3, 4, 38, 59–71
Marketing strategy, *see* Corporate social responsibilities, marketing strategy
Markowitz, S., 33, 41, 67
Miller, N. E., 41
Miller, S. M., 35
Minimum price policies, 4, 62, 73, 81, 82, 90–92, 102
Morbidity, 6, 9, 26, 32, 88
Mortality, 6, 9, 10, 13, 22, 23, 27, 32, 42, 47, 56, 63, 88, 90
Moskowitz, H., 54
Moskowitz, S., 26
Mullahy, J., 13, 66, 80, 88
Murphy, K. M., 34, 90

N
Nicotine, 1, 16, 24, 31, 40, 44, 47, 48, 50, 70

O
Operant conditioning, 16
Optimum Policy mix, 41

P
Pancreatic (acute and chronic), 16, 23
Pathways and progression of alcohol usage, 2, 11, 14, 15, 29, 101
Pharmacogenetics, 3, 43, 44
Phases and intervention, 2, 14
Pigovian tax, 87, 89
Policies, restrictive, alcohol consumption, 39, 62
Pregnancy, *see* Alcohol consumption, pregnancy
Price promotion, 3, 49, 53, 102
Prodromal phase, 14
Prohibition, *see* Alcohol, prohibition
Psychiatric morbidity, 26
Psycho-social effects of alcohol abuse, *see* Alcohol abuse, psycho-social effects

R
Randomized Breath Testing, 3, 40, 49, 54, 102
Rehm, J., 9, 16, 17, 20, 23, 24, 42, 90
Room, R., 20, 29

S
Sales, conditions of
  advertising ban of alcoholic beverages, 3, 44, 50, 56, 94, 102
  hours of opening, 3, 4, 49, 52
  markets of alcohol, 3, 39, 56, 61, 83
  outlets, location, density, 40, 49
  price promotion, discounts, 3, 49, 53, 102
  randomized breath testing, 3, 40, 49, 54, 102
Sales tax, 63, 74, 78
Science into practice, 41

Self-medication, *see* Alcohol abuse, self-medication
Self-regulation, alcohol industry, 4, 40, 52, 56, 57, 78, 85, 93, 94, 95, 96, 97, 98, 99
  See also Corporate social responsibilities, self-regulation
Sgontz, L. G., 86, 89
Sindelar, J. L., 66, 80, 88
Skeletal and muscular diseases, 18
Social problems, acute, chronic
  See also Alcohol abuse; Social problems, acute, chronic
Standard drink, 6, 7, 10, 23, 24
Stewardship, guided state, 40
Suicide, 2, 3, 9, 11, 13, 14, 21, 26, 27, 28

T

Taxation policies, 4, 34, 38, 50, 57, 76, 78, 80, 81, 84, 101, 102
  compared with minimum price policies, 4, 62, 73, 81, 82, 90, 91, 92, 102
Taxation, *see* Alcohol abuse, taxation
Treatment, effectiveness, *see* Alcohol abuse, treatment, effectiveness
Tuberculosis, 18, 20, 22

U

Utility, gaining, 86
  losing, 86

V

Violence, *see* Alcohol abuse, violence

W

Walsh, B., 13, 26, 27
Walsh, D., 13, 26, 27
Wernicke-Korsakoff syndrome, *see* Korsakoff-Wernicke syndrome
Willenbring, M. L., 32, 55
Withdrawal symptoms, 12, 14, 30, 38
World Health Organization, 6, 7, 8, 9, 18, 20, 22, 25, 30, 32, 40, 62, 96, 97, 99

CPSIA information can be obtained
at www.ICGtesting.com
Printed in the USA
LVHW071228210620
658633LV00037B/1644

9 783319 544243